LOVING YOURSELF
LOVING ANOTHER

You may also be interested in the following Relate titles published by Vermilion:

Better Relationships by Sarah Litvinoff

Staying Together by Susan Quilliam

Sex in Loving Relationships by Sarah Litvinoff

Starting Again by Sarah Litvinoff

Second Families by Suzie Hayman

Loving in Later Life by Suzy Powling and Marj Thoburn

Stop Arguing, Start Talking by Susan Quilliam

After the Affair by Julia Cole

To obtain a copy, simply telephone TBS Direct on 01206 255800

relate

LOVING YOURSELF LOVING ANOTHER

The importance of self-esteem for successful relationships

Julia Cole

Vermilion
LONDON

For Eileen

18 20 19 17

First published in 2001 by Vermilion,
an imprint of Ebury Publishing

A Random House Group company

Copyright © Julia Cole and Relate 2001

Julia Cole has asserted her right to be identified as the author of this work in
accordance with the Copyright, Designs and Patents Act 1988

The Random House Group Limited Reg. No. 954009

Addresses for companies within the Random House Group can be found at:
www.randomhouse.co.uk

A CIP catalogue record for this book is available from the British Library

ISBN 9780091856762

Copies are available at special rates for bulk orders. Contact the sales
development team on 020 7840 8487 for more information.

To buy books by your favourite authors and register for offers, visit
www.randomhouse.co.uk

Penguin Random House is committed to a sustainable future for
our business, our readers and our planet. This book is made from
Forest Stewardship Council® certified paper.

Printed and bound in Great Britain by Clays Ltd, St Ives plc

CONTENTS

ACKNOWLEDGEMENTS

I would like to express my warmest thanks to everyone who helped to make this book possible:

To Suzy Powling, Derek Hill and Sarah Bowler, previously of Relate, and Angela Sibson, Marj Thoburn and Sue Broome of Relate who supported and encouraged me in the writing of this book.

To Jacqueline Burns, Joanna Carreras and Kate Adams of Vermilion for all their hard work towards ensuring that *Loving Yourself, Loving Another* reached fruition.

To Jo Frank, my agent, for her wise advice and help in all my literary endeavours.

A thank you to all the couples whom I have counselled through Relate, and whose real-life experiences helped to inspire the content of this book.

And to my family, Peter, Adam and Hannah, for their understanding and loving support in all my work.

FOREWORD

If you do not love yourself, it is almost impossible to love another. Valuing your own abilities and attributes helps you to feel good about yourself. This can not only make you attractive to a partner, but will enable you to be part of a loving relationship that is secure and satisfying. From self-esteem comes couple-esteem. Couple-esteem can create a partnership that supports your relationship in work and home life, allowing you to feel free to enjoy life instead of finding yourself shoring up a troubled partnership.

This book is divided into two sections. The first section looks at different elements of self-esteem, dividing self-esteem into three different areas – the physical, mental and emotional self. This section contains several questionnaires that will help you to assess your personal level of self-esteem as well as offering suggestions for increasing self-esteem, and help in understanding why low self-esteem can develop. The different chapters in this section will also help you to: understand how self-esteem is formed, cope with anxiety, improve a poor body image and learn how to manage difficult emotions.

The second section discusses couple-esteem. Each chapter looks at a different aspect of couple relationships, including how to create couple-esteem and make it

work for you, sexual relationships and hurtful relationships. This section also offers new ways of managing
relationship problems, as well as celebrating positive
aspects of couple relationships.

Relate counsellors often report that lack of self-esteem
frequently underpins problem relationships. Arguments,
communication problems, depression and sexual difficulties can all stem from low self-esteem in one or both
partners. Chronic anxiety and stress can also indicate
low couple-esteem. The aim of this book is to offer a
practical guide to building positive self- and couple-
esteem across the whole of a partnership.

Before you read this book, ask yourself why you chose
it. Do you feel that your self-esteem is at a low ebb?
Would you like to know how to improve your sense of
self-worth? And would you like to understand how to
boost your couple-esteem? If you have answered yes to
these questions, then this is the book for you, but do not
forget that Relate is there for you if you need further
help. In a Relate study, 80 per cent of people who used
the agency said they were satisfied with the service they
received. Relate counsellors really can help you to resolve
relationship problems and regain a positive self-esteem.

Chapter 1

THE IMPORTANCE OF SELF-ESTEEM

Do you like yourself? Are you comfortable in your own skin? If you have picked up this book my guess is that sometimes you feel good about yourself and sometimes you do not. You may also find that when your self-esteem is low, your relationships with others – especially your partner – suffer. Many Relate counsellors say that a low sense of self-esteem in one, or both people, in a partnership is the single largest contribution to relationship problems. Low self-esteem in both partners can lead to a feeling that the relationship is lacking in some way, often leading to arguments and sometimes the breakdown of the relationship. This book will help you to understand more about the development of self-esteem, how to cultivate a sense of self-esteem that is appropriate for you and how to use this knowledge to improve your 'couple-esteem' – whether your relationship feels out of touch and under par or switched on and supportive.

WHAT IS SELF-ESTEEM?

Of course, what is actually meant by self-esteem often differs from person to person. For some people, low self-esteem comes from disliking their body shape. For others, it is caused by guilt about something they wish they had not done. High self-esteem can result from such diverse factors as enjoying work, running a marathon or becoming a parent.

But most people do not experience the soaring heights of euphoric self-esteem all the time. We all tend to go up and down on a graph that, spread over a period of time, would demonstrate that we have good days, weeks or months, and some less good times. If the ups and downs balance each other out most people would say that they feel OK about their life. If the downs outweigh the ups, we are likely to feel depressed and to find life very difficult to cope with. If the ups far outweigh the downs, we *could* be left feeling that we always had to live at this level. We might even fear that the euphoria of feeling this way might not be maintained, and spend a lot of time waiting for a fall. Most of us think of a mix of ups and downs as 'normal'.

WHY IS SELF-ESTEEM IMPORTANT?

The simple answer is that self-esteem is important because life is more pleasurable when we feel better about ourselves. This is absolutely true. Positive self-esteem can help us to enjoy the good things in life and have the energy to tackle the less good. But high or low self-esteem can also affect our health, our relationships with our families and work colleagues, and our attitude to everyday experiences. The woman who drives home from work having just learnt she is to be promoted will feel very different from the woman who has just learnt she is to be made redundant. The woman who is to lose her job may fume at traffic jams and be less attentive because she feels miserable than the woman who has been promoted who tolerates the traffic jam and feels great. A positive self-esteem can also help us to live in the present and look to the future, rather than be dogged by the weight of the past. A great deal of low self-esteem comes from feelings about the past – perceptions of negative messages from parents, poor attainment at school or failure in choice of career. If you continue to define yourself by what happened to you in the past, or to see yourself through another's eyes, you may find it very hard to feel happy about yourself. At its worst, low self-esteem can blacken your view of the world, preventing you from seizing opportunities or simply feeling contented. People who have felt this deep lack of self-esteem describe it as being rather like losing their sense of taste and smell. You may still eat, but there is no pleasure in eating. People with low self-esteem may go through the motions of their everyday life, but find no enjoyment in what they are doing. Low self-esteem de-sensitises you to the things you need – affection, joy, fun and supportive love. High self-esteem allows you to recognise these important elements in life and make the most of them.

WHAT AFFECTS SELF-ESTEEM?

How we feel about ourselves is determined by a huge number of variables. We tend to judge ourselves not only by our own values and ideas, but also by how others judge us. So self-esteem, high or low, can be affected by the following:

- *Gender: how we feel about being a man or a woman.* For instance, you may never have asked yourself if you are happy with the gender you are, but many transsexuals would say that their unhappiness with their gender contributed to a low self-image.
- *Age: how we feel about the age we are.* We live in a society that often focuses on youth to the detriment of the older (and sometimes wiser!). Thus older people may feel less valued and experience a lowering of self-esteem. We can also feel differently about our age depending on how we view being older or younger. The child may long to be an adult and free from restrictions. The adult may look back on childhood, envying the freedom from responsibility.
- *Social status and whether this has remained constant or changed.* For instance, we may feel good about a recent promotion or devastated by a redundancy. Where we live and the kind of house we buy, the car we drive and clothes we wear can all contribute to a feeling that we are doing well, or not so well, in life.
- *Cultural and ethnic background.* For instance, the young black man who is repeatedly insulted by white youths on the street where he lives may develop a low sense of self-esteem. Alternatively, the young French au pair who uses her language to develop French speaking skills in her young charges may feel good about herself as a result of sharing her native language and culture.
- *Physical appearance and body image.* This area is open to a number of different interpretations. For instance,

there is evidence to suggest that, at any one time in the UK, about 40 per cent of women are on a slimming diet of some kind. They may feel that their bodies are not acceptable because they do not conform to some fashion ideal. Alternatively, a man in a wheel-chair may feel completely comfortable with his body, although others may consider him to be dis-advantaged.

- *General lifestyle.* We may enjoy sports or days out with the family and feel that these help to keep us sane. Or we may experience life as stressful and unful-filling, devoid of such pleasures, which can lead to a lack of self-esteem.
- *Position in the family.* We may feel valued and loved by our family or uncared for and rejected.
- *Relationships to others in the world around us.* If we get on well with others at work and feel supported in our partnerships and families then we are likely to have good self-esteem. If we continually battle against an unsympathetic employer or are going through a rough patch with a partner or family member, self-esteem may take a battering.
- *Spiritual attitude to life.* Many people have a belief system that helps to sustain them throughout life. For some this is overtly religious. For others it is more about a code of ethics and morality that they choose to live by. For instance, the woman who thinks stealing is always wrong may find her self-esteem plummets when she discovers her teenage son has been shop-lifting, blaming herself for his shortcomings.
- *Health and wellbeing.* Health or sickness can affect your self-esteem. Pain, disability and the exhaustion of

struggling with health problems can make you feel unhappy about yourself, especially if your illness does not appear to have a resolution. It may also alter your self-image in a way that you dislike. For instance, women who lose a breast through cancer often experience extreme sadness at the change to their body, and feel that their personal sexual identity is threatened.

DEVELOPING SELF-ESTEEM

It is not always possible to maintain high self-esteem throughout life. Facing the reality of events and developing useful strategies to manage them is part of maturation. Healthy self-esteem is composed of:

1 The ability to accept those things about yourself that you know might be very hard, or impossible, to change. These might include being short when you want to be tall, or being an only child when you always wanted brothers and sisters.
2 The willingness to improve those areas that might be amenable to change, such as educational attainment, and/or coming to terms with how you are – sometimes regardless of the judgement of others.

Most people go through phases of wanting to change things that are unchangeable and wishing for the impossible whilst avoiding making changes to those things that could be changed! This seems to be part of being human and could simply be the triumph of hope over experience as well as plain stubbornness!

This kind of perverseness is quite common – for

example, Mike wanted to be fit so that he could run in a mini-marathon with his son but refused to give up smoking even though he would probably never keep up with his son while still smoking. Occasionally, however, this perverseness can be uplifting and useful. There are lots of examples of people who were told, after an accident, that they would never walk again who got back on their feet by sheer determination. Some para and tetraplegics – notably Christopher Reeve, 'Superman' in the films of the same name – believe that they will, one day, walk again, although research in this area of medicine is painfully slow. Holding onto a belief that things will change can get people through very tough times and improve their self-esteem when there is very little else to be cheerful about. At a deeper level, fighting for something in this way can actually help to alter the way we feel about the problem we are facing and prevent it dragging us down to the depths of despair.

It has become commonplace to talk about this kind of behaviour as 'denial' – the treatment for which is to face the truth about everything that is unpleasant. But a certain type of denial can be beneficial: it can allow people to see the problem, but focus on the positive and come through the event. This explains why some people, in the face of great adversity, somehow still manage to live fulfilling and satisfying lives. Lacking this 'denial' attribute may explain why some people can be completely floored by a minor setback, which sometimes results in depression and low self-esteem.

So how do these differences in self-esteem, self-determination and optimism develop? And what contributes to their maintenance throughout life? Positive self-esteem is probably determined by many different factors. Here are some factors that point to a high sense of self-esteem:

- **Inheritance.** It is likely that a person's ability to feel good about himself or herself is partly genetic – that is, inherited from their parents. We all know someone who seems to bounce back after problems or who retains a high sense of self-esteem even when faced with something that would floor other people. If their parent(s) also have this attribute, or there are marked similarities between their attitude and others in their family history, they may simply be lucky enough to have a predisposition to feeling good about themselves.
- **Upbringing.** This is a key area for the building of self-esteem. Children who are given positive messages about themselves from family, friends, teachers and others tend to grow up to have a lively sense of self-esteem. They are likely to be able to manage tough times because they feel secure about their own place in the world and are able to take on new challenges more joyfully than those who are less secure. Children who are put down, criticised, mocked and generally made to feel of little worth are much more likely to become adults who suffer from low self-esteem. There will be more about this crucial area later in the book, but it is worth mentioning it here as it is one of the most important components of self-esteem.
- **Life experiences.** From childhood onwards we all go through a variety of life events. We may have brothers and sisters or none, experience bereavement, parental divorce or family money problems. As we grow up, all of our life experiences contribute to our self-esteem. For some, passing or failing exams can

have a strong effect as well as things like finding the right partner, choosing the right career, feeling accepted in a strange part of the country, and so on. How we respond to different life experiences is also important in establishing self-esteem. If our upbringing helped us to feel secure and good about ourselves, we will be better able to cope with the slings and arrows that life throws at us than if we started out feeling insecure. Some life experiences, however, can be so traumatic that they may leave a profound legacy of low self-esteem. I would include physical, mental and sexual abuse in this category as well as losing a parent or other close relative. However, other positive life experiences can help to dampen down the unhappy effects of a traumatic past. Building a loving relationship, finding supportive friends or working in a fascinating job can all go a long way towards improving self-esteem and counteracting the negative effects of past unhappy experiences.

- **Individual character.** Your character and personality are the result of a mixture of nature and nurture – what you have inherited from parents and what you have experienced in life. For instance, Tina is a shy woman who finds it hard to initiate conversation and often lurks in the corner at parties. From the outside, strangers can dismiss her as 'boring', but those who get to know her tell a different story. She can relate a witty story with panache and is fiercely loyal to those she feels confident with. Tina's mother was also shy, but warm and affectionate towards Tina. Tina recognises that her shyness in social situations is probably inherited from her mother (she may also have learnt to be shy by observing her mother's behaviour). But she has an inner store of self-esteem resulting from her mother's care for her as she grew up. Self-esteem can often be lowered or boosted according to how others respond to your personality and how you regard yourself. Tina is a different person in the voluntary role she undertakes at weekends. She works in a hospice with terminally ill people where her quiet and calm nature encourages people to talk to her about their fears and concerns. So what seems a handicap in one area of life can pay dividends in another. Tina accepts her shyness partly because she knows that this quality allows her to deal empathetically with the patients at the hospice. Her self-esteem is intact.

- **The influence of others.** This is not an easy area to discuss in the context of self-esteem. By 'others' I mean those not in your family as we have already looked at some issues concerning family upbringing. I am thinking of work colleagues, friends and other people you meet in your normal day. This is rather a 'chicken and egg' situation as regards self-esteem. If you are already suffering from low self-esteem – perhaps because of a difficult situation at home or feeling unwell – you might interpret everything that your work colleague says as a put-down. Luke was in the middle of a messy divorce. He had moved out of the family home and was badly missing his two young sons. His colleague, Eve, asked to meet him to talk over a project that was way overdue for completion. Luke interpreted everything Eve said about the problems with the project as his fault. In fact, Eve was simply trying to sort out what had gone wrong and did not see Luke as the problem at all. Luke ended the meeting feeling dreadful and went home to his bed-sit wondering if life was worth carrying on with. Luke's stressful home circumstances made him interpret Eve's comments as a personal attack when no criticism had been implied.

Alternatively, the behaviour of others can lower your self-esteem so that you come to believe you really are useless (or whatever they say you are). For example, Elaine worked in a factory and was part of a small team making panels for machinery. An older woman, who seemed to go out of her way to rubbish whatever she did, supervised her. Elaine found this really battered her self-esteem. Even when she was at home with her family she found herself doubting whether she could do simple things such as cooking the family their evening meal. In fact, the criticism affected her so badly that she began to make mistakes at work, giving the woman more reason to shout at her. Elaine felt caught in a vicious circle from which there was no escape. The rest of Elaine's team had all suffered the cruelty of the supervisor and were afraid to stand up for Elaine. One or two were even secretly relieved that Elaine was acting as the team scapegoat as it allowed them to avoid being drawn into the firing line. Eventually Elaine asked to be transferred to a different department where a new manager helped her to realise that she had good work skills and that her low self-esteem was mainly due to the repeated emotional knocks she had taken from her old supervisor.

Sometimes low self-esteem originates from an expectation that things will not improve so that you look for criticism and negativity where there is none, or your self-esteem may be lowered by the behaviour of another person. Of course, it can be a blending of both of these, but it is important to understand this difference when thinking about the nature of self-esteem. Many people have a tendency to blame themselves when they actually need to take a wider view of what has contributed to low (or high) self-esteem.

HOW THESE INFLUENCES AFFECT RELATIONSHIPS

All of these influences can have an impact on our choice of partner, how we feel about and react to them and whether we develop a long-term relationship. This book is not only about individual self-esteem, but also about the role that self-esteem plays in personal relationships. When self-esteem is low, your partnership can suffer. If your self-esteem is high it can help your partnership to feel satisfying.

When two people make a commitment to each other they usually find that their moods and emotions rub off on each other. If one is happy, so often is the other. If one is depressed, it can lower the mood of the partner. Most people know this, even if at only a subconscious level. They may watch their partner closely, looking for changes in mood. Some couples have very acute antennae for this variation in self-esteem. They can almost tell how their partner is feeling when they walk through the door at the end of a working day. For others it can depend on particular circumstances, perhaps if the pair have spent a lot or a little time together, for instance. It is not unusual to find that one partner expects the other to be very aware of the minutiae of their feelings only to discover that they simply have not noticed. This might make the person feel that their partner does not care about them rather than accepting that people can have different approaches to similar concerns. In the second section of this book you will find more information about 'couple-esteem' – what it is, how to cultivate it and what to do if problems develop that lower a sense of shared esteem.

SELF-ESTEEM IN RELATIONSHIPS – WHY IS IT IMPORTANT?

Feeling confident about yourself is not only important for yourself but also has an impact on couple relationships. If you can maintain a healthy sense of self-esteem it will spill over into your partnership. You will also feel better able to support your partner if they are feeling low, and survive setbacks without thinking the end of the world is coming. Over a period of time you will feel like a team – pulling together to manage your life together. If one, or both, of you lacks a sense of reasonable self-esteem, every unfortunate event will feel like a major stumbling block. You may also end up feeling exhausted because you try hard to support each other, but never deal with the problem at hand. Lack of self-esteem can also colour events that should be enjoyable. Gradually, you may both begin to feel that the relationship is stagnant and unsupportive. This may not be true. It could be that you or your partner feels so bad about himself or herself that the relationship just *feels* blighted.

Of course, there will be plenty of times when one of you feels OK while the other feels miserable or anxious. Most people would agree that one of the good things about loving partnerships is that partners support each other through difficult times, as well as sharing the celebrations of the happy times. Couples who possess a strong sense of individual self-esteem usually feel better able to give this kind of support than couples who have low self-esteem. If only one partner suffers from low self-esteem, the other may feel resentment when their partner is unable to give help or advice because they lack the personal resources to do so.

A good analogy is to imagine two tall pots filled to the brim with water. A pipe continually flows into the pots, keeping them full, so that people taking cups of water from them hardly notice any change in the level of the water. This shows how a couple with high self-esteem functions. Coping with a difficult time makes some difference, but not enough to make the couple's emotional well run dry. Now imagine that something goes wrong with the water supply to one of the pots. The supply is now routed through the good pot to the defective one. This makes a significant difference to the water in the good pot, but it is still not empty. One person with high self-esteem can support the other for a time, but perhaps not indefinitely. If the water supply to the working pot should falter, it would be very hard for the defective one to keep going.

Some couples encounter a variation of this pheno-menon. They may feel that no matter how much support and care they lavish on their partner, it makes little difference because it appears to drain away as fast as it is given. Their partner resembles a colander. So, positive and negative self-esteem can make all the difference in couple relationships, sometimes spelling the difference between success and failure.

Unfortunately, lowered self-esteem can become a downward spiral because once a person begins to feel unhappy they may behave in a way that makes the bad feeling worse. For example, Mark gained weight after he stopped playing rugby due to an injury. He disliked his weight gain and started to avoid going to the club nights out or taking his partner, Kerry, out for any social events. Mark compensated for his change in lifestyle by comfort eating at home. He gained even more weight and his self-esteem plummeted further. Kerry began to won-der if he was avoiding being with her, culminating in her feeling confused and upset. Mark and Kerry began to argue and soon found they were feeling very fed-up with each other. Eventually, Mark admitted his feelings about himself. Kerry told him how much she loved him, no matter what his size, and agreed to help him to eat more sensibly. They also made a resolution to go out together more.

This kind of downward spiral can cause more damage if both partners are suffering from low self-esteem and have little to give each other. Alison and Simon found they had little to give each other from an emotional point of view after their shared business failed. Their small tool rental firm had represented a dream they had both held of running their own business. But the debts soon began to mount up and they had to admit defeat. Alison and Simon each privately held themselves to blame. Alison felt she should have worked harder to market the business, while Simon felt he had not handled the financial side as well as he could. They both became depressed, and found supporting each other through their unhappiness almost impossible. Slowly they drifted apart, each wrapped up in their own sadness and unable to talk about how they were feeling. After almost a year, Alice left Simon, returning to live with a friend she had shared a house with before she and Simon moved in together. It took a long time before Alice was able to feel OK about herself, the disappointment of a broken relationship and the failed business. Simon became so miserable that he considered suicide, but was pulled back from the brink of despair by a friend who supported him during the loss of the business and the breakdown of his relationship with Alice.

You can read more about the role of self-esteem in relationships in Section Two of this book – *Loving Another*.

THE ROAD TO SELF-ESTEEM

This chapter has been aimed at introducing some ideas that will be explored later in the book as you read on. It is, however, important to point out that self-esteem is like a road, not an island. The journey of growing to love yourself is never finished. We tend to imagine that there is a destination that once arrived at will be the end point

– that we will somehow find life perfect and feel great about ourselves if we can only just reach this point. Thousands of pounds are poured into promoting this idea through advertising. From the perfect bra to the most exciting car, we are encouraged to believe that ideal self-esteem can be achieved by owning (or emulating) whatever the adman wants us to desire. The problem is that once we own or achieve the object of desire we are likely to realise that it does not actually make us feel wonderful about ourselves.

In reality, acquiring positive self-esteem is a journey, full of meandering twists and turns because of the nature of change. Every person experiences change. How we learn to respond to this and understand it can have a crucial effect on our self-esteem. Loving yourself as you age, make relationships, suffer ill health or gain good health, become a parent or grandparent and experience the ups and downs of life is as important as choosing a healthy diet. Self-esteem is not selfish or self-centred. It maintains your mental, physical and emotional health and allows you to enjoy your journey on the road of life.

Section I

LOVING
YOURSELF

Chapter 2

QUESTIONNAIRES

In this section of the book you will read about the key elements of personal self-esteem – what it is and how to maintain it. The section breaks down into four chapters (including this one) that describe the different parts of self-esteem. This chapter will act as an introduction to the three following chapters which deal with:

- The perception of your physical self and how you feel about your body
- Understanding your emotions and their role in your sense of self-esteem
- The role of mental health, including the impact of stress and anxiety on self-esteem

This chapter contains a number of questionnaires that link up with these chapters. Completing them will enable you apply the information to your personal situation and feelings. For instance, you may discover that you have high self-esteem at work but a lower self-esteem in your family life. The questionnaires may reveal whether this is likely be temporary or a long-standing problem that needs attention. You can also use the questionnaires to help you to make sense of your general attitude to yourself, and learn to compensate for inappropriately negative thoughts or feelings. The questionnaires cover the three areas outlined in Chapters 3, 4, and 5 – your physical self, your emotional responses and your mental health. There will be some areas of overlap. This is because it is not possible to break a human being into neatly defined parts! We are all more than the sum of our parts. All the three areas defined above influence each other. A job that is full of stress and overwork might cause you to fall prey to a series of minor infections, making you feel bad-tempered and grumpy. In this case all three areas – physical, mental and emotional – will be influenced, culminating in lowered self-esteem all round. However, the questionnaire might allow you to pinpoint particular problems in one area that are clearly influencing other areas. Clearing up one issue might result in positive changes in other areas. In the example above, cutting back on too much work, for example, could have prevented problems in other areas of self-esteem.

FILLING IN THE QUESTIONNAIRES

You have probably filled in loads of quizzes and questionnaires in magazines and newspapers just for a laugh. But these questionnaires are different. Here are some suggestions to help you to fill them in effectively.

- Put some time aside for the task. You may not want to do all of them at once, so decide how long you might need. I suggest at least half an hour for each questionnaire.
- Make yourself comfortable. You may wish to sit on your favourite chair or at the kitchen table. Do whatever feels right for you.

- Ensure you have peace and quiet. Disturbances from partner, children, telephone or TV and radio will prevent you from concentrating on your responses.
- Answer as truthfully as you can. You may want to deliberate over some answers, while others come to you quickly. Just try to be honest and you will find the experience of completing the questionnaires interesting and stimulating. You may wish to keep your answers on a separate sheet of paper to ensure confidentiality.
- Do not show other people how you have answered unless you really feel you want to. It is not unusual for a partner to want to know what you are filling in and to read your answers, perhaps in an effort to find out some 'secret' about you. But my advice is to preserve your privacy and think through your answers. If you then wish to share your thoughts, that is, of course, your choice.

QUESTIONNAIRE 1 – THE PHYSICAL SELF

Tick the column that most applies to your personal experience in answer to the question or statement in the first column. For instance, if you agree that you feel at ease with your current body shape, tick the appropriate box.

This questionnaire aims to help you to understand how you feel about your body. You may discover that you care for and respect your body, or that you often push your body beyond its limitations. There are no 'right' or 'wrong' answers – just answers that you feel describe your current approach to your body. As you complete the questionnaire, notice how you are feeling. Are some questions easier to answer than others? Do you find it hard to know where to put your response? Are you surprised by any answer you have given? You may find that you feel a bit sceptical about filling in the questionnaire, but this is natural, as it may be the first time that you have completed a set of questions on this aspect of yourself.

———————— *Questionnaire 1* ————————
THE PHYSICAL SELF

Question / Statement	Strongly agree	Agree	Do not agree	Strongly disagree
I feel at ease with my current body shape.				
I treat my body with respect.				
I often wish my body was different in some way.				
I have a physical disability that I feel at ease with.				
I have a physical disability that I feel has a negative effect on me.				
I care about what others think about my physical appearance.				

Question/ Statement	Strongly agree	Agree	Do not agree	Strongly disagree
I sometimes feel constrained in sexual relationships because I dislike my body shape.				
My body is a source of pleasure to me.				
I dislike the way that others sometimes react to my body.				
I am proud of my ethnic background.				
I dislike the way that other people respond to my ethnicity.				
I like the way that people respond to my ethnicity.				
My body has changed a lot over the years.				
I like the way my body has changed during my lifetime.				
I enjoy being a man or a woman.				
I do not enjoy being a man or a woman.				

Question / Statement	Strongly agree	Agree	Do not agree	Strongly disagree
I have had an illness/accident that has changed my body in some way.				
I am comfortable with the changes that have occurred to my body.				
For women: I have had few/no problems with my menstrual cycle or fertility.				
For men: I have had few/no problems with my fertility.				
For women: Problems with my fertility have changed my view of the way my body functions.				
For men: Problems with my fertility have changed my view of the way my body functions.				
For women who have experienced childbirth: Having a child changed the way I viewed my body.				

Question/ Statement	Strongly agree	Agree	Do not agree	Strongly disagree
I know I sometimes endanger my physical health by drinking/smoking/ taking drugs/taking risks, etc.				
I would like to stop behaving in a way that endangers my health.				
If I have a minor illness I take appropriate steps to care for myself.				
I do not always care appropriately for myself if I am ill.				
I eat a reasonably balanced diet.				
I sometimes eat or approach eating in a way that is unhealthy (eg: eat too little, take laxatives, etc).				
I sometimes binge on foods.				
I take appropriate exercise for my age and circumstances.				

Question / Statement	Strongly agree	Agree	Do not agree	Strongly disagree
I probably do not take enough exercise for my age and circumstances.				
I exercise a lot – perhaps too much for my age and circumstances.				
I feel in touch with my body's needs for rest and recuperation.				
I sleep well and rarely suffer from insomnia.				
I often have trouble sleeping and find this disturbing.				
I often (more than twice a month) suffer from:				
• stress headaches/ migraines				
• aches and pains – especially neck, shoulder and back aches				
• stomach ache or digestive problems				
• tiredness or exhaustion.				

Now that you have completed this questionnaire, read back through your answers. Unlike other questionnaires of this type, I am not going to suggest you add up scores or try to decide if you are fit, unfit, happy or unhappy. Instead, look carefully at which box you have ticked. Ask yourself what each answer means to you. Some questions/statements are vaguer than others. For instance, the first statement asks if you feel 'at ease with your body'. Only you can decide what 'at ease' means. For you, it may mean that given your personal circumstances you are relatively at ease. Or you may personally feel very ill at ease, even if to others you seem perfectly content. Other questions/statements are more specific. For example, the last part of the questionnaire asks you to decide if you have regular stress headaches. You will need to work out if you do or do not have headaches more than twice a month.

This questionnaire is designed to help you to look at your body from several different perspectives:

- Your general feelings about your body – whether you feel content with its shape, strength and so on.
- Your feelings about your body as a source of sexual pleasure – how you feel about your body during sexual relationships, as well as your perception of how your partner might feel about your body.
- Your feeling about your body as representative of your culture and ethnicity – for some, this is a source of pride. For others there may be mixed feelings as their ethnicity may invite prejudice or abuse from others.
- Your feeling about your body as you grow older. Even if you consider yourself to be young, you will still

have experienced changes to your body as you have grown up. For example, changes may result from becoming pregnant, giving birth or breast-feeding. Some women feel more in touch with their body during these changes; other women feel alienated and upset at the profound changes their body experiences during pregnancy.

- Your feeling about being a man or a woman. This may seem rather a surprising thought, but not everybody is comfortable with the sex and gender they find themselves assigned to.
- Your feelings about any changes you have faced, including illnesses and accidents. These kinds of change can have a far-reaching effect on an individual, radically changing how they feel about their body.
- Your feelings about how you take care of your body – including diet and exercise, as well as any form of abuse, such as drugs or alcohol.
- Signs and symptoms that you are pushing your body too much, such as headaches, muscle aches and so on. (If you have identified any physical symptoms that worry you, seek the help of your GP or a medical professional.)

Case Study

As 36-year-old Eddie completed the 'Body' questionnaire he began to realise that he often pushed himself to 'perform' when he was tired or unable to give of his best. Eddie is a sales rep for a medical company, frequently spending hours driving around his sector of the country selling medical products to health centres and hospitals. He decided that he often covers up just how tired he really is, because he wants to be seen to do well at his job. After completing the questionnaire, Eddie found that he was not using appropriate time to rest and recuperate. In fact, he was forcing himself to maintain a high octane social life, including sports and social events, that often left him facing Monday mornings exhausted rather than ready for the week's work.

In Chapter 3 there are suggestions for improving body awareness and self-esteem. You can go straight to Chapter 3 now or complete the other questionnaires in this chapter before reading on.

——————— *Questionnaire 2* ———————
THE EMOTIONAL SELF

Question/ Statement	Strongly agree	Agree	Do not agree	Strongly disagree
I am usually aware of my emotions in any given situation.				
I am often unaware of my emotions in any given situation.				
I can usually control my feelings/ emotions.				
I find it hard to control my emotions.				
Others are usually able to know what I am feeling.				

Question / Statement	Strongly agree	Agree	Do not agree	Strongly disagree
Others may find it difficult to know what I am feeling.				
I can reveal my emotions/feelings to those close to me.				
I do not often reveal my feelings/ emotions to others.				
Too much is made of being emotional.				
Most people could benefit from being more open about their feelings.				
I pay attention to what I am feeling and use this information to help me to make sense of life.				
My emotions do not seem to impact much on my normal life.				
I know that I have been loved.				
I know that I am loved today.				
I can let others know I love them.				

Question/ Statement	Strongly agree	Agree	Do not agree	Strongly disagree
Other people often tell me they love me.				
I am capable of expressing anger.				
I am sometimes unhappy about the way I express my anger.				
I do not often show my anger, even if I know I feel angry.				
I can show anger without violence (physical or emotional).				
I am sometimes aggressively angry.				
I avoid any expression of anger, by others or myself.				
I would describe myself as able to show affection to those I care about.				
I find it difficult to show affection to those I care about.				
I am probably more of an introvert than an extrovert.				

Question / Statement	Strongly agree	Agree	Do not agree	Strongly disagree
I am probably more of an extrovert than an introvert.				
I often share with others what I feel.				
I find it hard to share what I feel.				
I can be jealous in certain situations.				
I am not usually jealous of others.				
I am not usually nervous in new situations.				
I know when I feel afraid.				
I am not usually aware of feeling afraid.				
I feel that my emotions are controlled.				
I sometimes feel overwhelmed by my emotional responses.				
I regard my emotions/ feelings as an important part of my personality.				
The ability to experience emotion enhances my normal life.				
Feelings and emotions sometimes get in the way of my normal life.				

As with the questionnaire on your physical self, read back through your answers on emotions and feelings. Do not try to make a judgement about whether it is 'right' for you to agree or disagree with a particular statement. Notice if any question was particularly difficult or surprising. If you have never asked yourself a particular question, think about what it may mean to you to have faced the issue. Some people find that their emotional responses are determined by where they are and who they are with – it might be OK to weep in front of a romantic film with your partner, but not with your boss! Not all the questions will seem to apply to you. It's OK not to have strong feelings about all the questions, but you may feel surprised at what you discover about yourself as you fill in the questionnaire.

The 'emotions' questionnaire is designed to help you to think about your emotions on several different levels. Here are the main areas covered by the questionnaire:

- Your awareness of your usual emotional state and how much this affects your life. Some of the questions also ask you to make a judgement about how you think your emotions impact on others.
- Your understanding about how you use your emotions to feed back into your everyday behaviour and decision making.
- Your experience of specific feelings and emotions – including love and affection, anger, fear and jealousy. There are sections on how you usually handle these emotions. Some statements ask you to make a

judgement about how you see yourself – introvert or extrovert, for example.

- Your response to the way emotions affect your everyday life. Some people feel that emotions are an aid to everyday experiences. Others feel that emotions cloud the ability to make reasoned decisions.

Case Study

Ellen, 54, found filling in the 'emotion' questionnaire difficult. She saw herself as an emotional person, often describing herself as someone who 'wore their heart on their sleeve'. Despite this, she had never asked herself what her emotions meant to her and what kind of role they played in her daily life. She was puzzled that she found herself agreeing strongly that she was often overwhelmed by her emotions, but also felt they played little useful role in her life. On reflection, she felt that her emotions, although often powerful, tended to sweep her along rather than help her to make decisions.

Chapter 4 provides help in understanding the role of the emotions and dealing with emotions that can be overwhelming or be hard to access. You can go straight to Chapter 4 now to understand more about emotions and self-esteem, or complete the final questionnaire before reading on.

——————— *Questionnaire 3* ———————
THE MENTAL HEALTH SELF

Question/ Statement	Strongly agree	Agree	Do not agree	Strongly disagree
I consider myself to have good mental health.				
My mood is usually the same from day to day.				
My mood varies from day to day.				
I feel low at least once in a day.				
I feel low about once a week.				
I feel low less than once a week.				
I can be easily undermined by minor setbacks.				
I am usually a confident person in everyday life.				
I can feel happy at least once a day.				
I feel happy about once a week.				
I feel happy less than once a week.				

Question / Statement	Strongly agree	Agree	Do not agree	Strongly disagree
I am sometimes anxious about my everyday life.				
I am sometimes so anxious it interferes with everyday life on a regular basis.				
I find I worry about events.				
I feel I worry more than is helpful to me.				
I think I live a stressful lifestyle.				
My stress is chiefly caused by:				
• my domestic circumstances				
• my work environment				
• my family life				
• my relationship with my partner.				
I often blame myself for things that go wrong, even if it is possible that it has no connection with me.				

Question/ Statement	Strongly agree	Agree	Do not agree	Strongly disagree
I sometimes blame others for things I should take responsibility for.				
I often feel tired and unable to cope with life.				
I often feel lonely.				
I have received medical treatment for a mental health concern.				
I often feel depressed.				
I tend to be a pessimist.				
I tend to be an optimist.				
I have recently been through a traumatic life change.				
I have experienced a traumatic life event at some point in the past *(bereavement, divorce, loss of job, accidents, etc)*.				
I generally approach life with a positive attitude.				

Question/ Statement	Strongly agree	Agree	Do not agree	Strongly disagree
I tend to think that things will turn out for the best.				
I accept life as it comes.				
I am the kind of person who likes to plan everything.				
I tend to worry if I do not know what is going to happen.				
I do not like surprises!				
I often work (paid or unpaid) long hours.				
My work hours often mean I have little time for rest and recuperation.				
I sometimes feel underused and bored in my everyday life.				
I feel I cope well with change.				
When a change comes, I usually find it relatively easy to adapt to that change.				

Question/ Statement	Strongly agree	Agree	Do not agree	Strongly disagree
I tend to find change disconcerting and like things to stay the same.				
I find communicating my ideas and feelings to others reasonably easy.				
I often find it hard to communicate my thoughts and feelings to others.				
I have considered ending my life.				
I have sometimes felt isolated from my friends and relations.				
I have supportive friends and relations who I can turn to if I need help.				
I have a partner who supports me.				
On balance, I have a good working (paid or unpaid) environment.				

Once you have completed this questionnaire, read back through your answers. As you do this, try to remember if any of the questions sparked a particular response. Did you find yourself feeling uncomfortable or particularly pleased about any of your answers? Did answering any of them evoke any particular feelings of surprise? For instance, you may have felt surprised at agreeing that you usually handle change well, when you sometimes felt that you found change difficult. Sometimes, answering a questionnaire in this way can be a real eye-opener. You might find that you answer questions in a way that is unexpected. These feelings often come from deep inside, circumventing the usual emotional and logic filters that we all use in everyday life.

This questionnaire is designed to encourage you to reflect on your general mental health. It is not intended to diagnose specific mental illnesses. If any of the answers have given you cause for concern, seek help from your GP. Here are the main areas the questionnaire covers:

- Issues concerning mood and your usual 'background' feelings. Most people go through different phases of mood according to their age, circumstances, gender and culture. For example, your 'background' mood may be influenced by particular circumstances, such as worrying about your family or job security. You may experience moods that are connected with your biological functioning – women may suffer from PMT or mood changes during the menopause, for instance. Some people's mood stays more or less the same each day, while others feel it varies considerably from day to day. There is no right or wrong mood state, although if you feel stuck in a depressive mood for weeks you may wish you could change this.

- Concerns about stress and anxiety. Stress in modern life is thought to be linked to an increase in the numbers of people suffering from depression and other mental illnesses. Sources of stress can be related to a number of different situations – work, home, personal circumstances. The questionnaire asks you to reflect on whether particular situations seem to lead to your personal experience of stress. Taking inappropriate responsibility for, or assigning inappropriate responsibility to others, can also be a symptom of stress and low self-esteem.

- Potential concerns arising from particular life events (such as bereavement) or feelings of isolation and loneliness.

- Your personal view of your general mental attitude. You may see yourself as optimistic or pessimistic, accepting or challenging of life. You may also like to be a careful planner or have a spontaneous disposition. Of course, most people are a mix of these differing attitudes, so your questionnaire may have ticks in the 'agree' columns of several seemingly opposite views. This is to be expected, and probably indicates a balance in your general attitudes.

Case Study

Lily, 42, completed the questionnaire shortly after she discovered that her husband had been having an affair. She found that the affair had had a deeper effect on her mental attitude than she had imagined, although they were trying to rebuild their marriage after the affair had ended. Lily would have previously described herself as a happy-go-lucky kind of person, but found herself ticking the 'agree strongly' boxes that asked if she was frequently unhappy or sad. She agreed that she was under stress and often more anxious than she had been before she discovered the affair. She recognised that she had been in a particularly difficult phase of life, but was still taken aback by the self-discovery of her feelings and mental attitude.

WHY COMPLETE THE QUESTIONNAIRES?

One of the dangers of a book on self-esteem is that you, the reader, may believe that there is an ideal sense of self-esteem that this book can somehow teach you. Once learnt, you may hope that you will feel OK for ever, never needing to attend to your self-esteem again. The truth is that you need to go on paying attention to your physical, emotional and mental self-esteem all your life, making adjustments as you change and mature.

The questionnaires are deliberately designed to help you to think about how you feel on a daily basis as well as offering a wider view of your self-esteem. Some of the questions are not in neat sections, and may seem out of order, but this is to help you to answer from the heart. This is often more easily done if you are not overly prepared for the next question, even slightly taken by surprise. As you fill in the boxes, you will learn about your personal responses to different questions. Many of these questions will be new to you; you may never have been asked them, even by your nearest and dearest. This is why it is useful to ask yourself these questions as you begin to think about your personal self-esteem. Facing them and considering what your answers tell you about yourself will help you to make changes for the better, or to accept that some changes may be very small.

Using the questionnaires in this way should give you a window on an aspect of yourself that you may never have considered in the past. This may be a positive experience, allowing you to see that although your sense of physical self-esteem is not great, mentally and emotional you feel stable and secure. Alternatively, you could realise that you need to develop your self-esteem in all three areas and that you have denied this, even to yourself.

Thinking about your self-esteem in this way gives you a new chance:

- A chance to review how you respond to events and situations
- A chance to take a deep breath and really look at yourself
- A chance to be honest about the things you might change
- A chance to understand how your personal self-esteem impacts on your relationships at home and in other situations
- And a real chance to use this book to alter these if you need and want to.

The next three chapters will allow you to use your reflections and discoveries from the questionnaires in greater depth. They will also explore the three areas of self-esteem in greater detail, offering practical help for understanding and solving particular problems in physical, emotional and mental self-esteem.

Chapter 3

LEARNING TO LOVE YOUR PHYSICAL SELF

What was your last New Year resolution? To lose weight? To stop eating chocolate? To get fitter? Thousands of people make New Year resolutions to deal with perceived problems with their body. Some pinpoint a particular problem, such as weight or body shape; others pinpoint habits that are bad for the health, such as smoking. Many 'get fit' regimes last until the third week of January and then peter out as determination and resolve begin to falter.

LEARNING ABOUT OUR BODIES

It seems as if we dislike our bodies more as we grow older. Small children usually accept their bodies for what they are – vehicles for enjoying all our five senses. They do not worry about whether their romper suit makes their bum look big or if their bald head is attractive or not! They use their body without awareness of these adult perceptions and seem to have a lot more fun doing it than most adults. The point here is not so much that they love their bodies (or even have any notion of *disliking* them), they just accept them. It is only as children grow older that they learn to tease the fat child or the child with glasses. This may be in imitation of older children and adults, who make judgements about others and give voice to their prejudices. It is also possible that there is an in-built human response to any difference from 'the home tribe'. In other words, children may look for similarities and differences in others in order to protect themselves from the threat of the unknown. If there is any truth in this theory, it has developed, in our civilised societies, into a sophisticated art form that can hurt anybody who has ever known the pain and isolation of appearing 'different'. Nowhere is this clearer than in how we look. First impressions can often be hard to overcome. Our personal prejudices (and we all have them, even if we would like to think we do not) can blight or enliven first meetings, and a great deal of this is connected to our bodies – their shape, age, colour, disability, and so on.

BODY ATTITUDES

Your body is both you and not-you. We all inhabit our bodies and they are who we are, but most people also experience their bodies as external to themselves. Try this – hold your hand up in front of you. You know you are looking at it, but it is both part of you and yet outside of your self. If your hand was lost because of an accident or illness you would still be you, although your view of yourself might have to adapt to this unfortunate loss. It is this 'me, but not me', view of our bodies that can contribute to problems with how we view our bodies. We might decide to ascribe all our problems to our lack of muscle tone or small breasts, reasoning that changing these will give us the life we want. To add to this love-hate relationship with our bodies, it *is* possible to change our bodies in a multiplicity of ways. We can gain or lose weight, cut and dye our hair, have tattoos or body piercing, take exercise or become a couch potato, and indulge in numerous other body-changing activities such as taking drugs or smoking (although these can also affect the inner self as well as our appearance). So not only are we affected *by* our body, we can also affect *it*, often according to the vagaries of fashion. If you are a Reubens woman in a Twiggy world, you may want a differently shaped body, but this is only because of living at a certain time in history, not because there is anything inherently wrong or ugly about your body. In fact, all body shapes and sizes are neutral – neither good nor bad. In the main, it is the attitudes of society towards the body that shape how we feel about our own body. The only exception to this general observation is in the field of medicine. Some medical experts have found links between particular body shapes and susceptibility to certain diseases, but this still does not necessarily make your body acceptable or unacceptable – just part of who you are.

USING YOUR 'BODY' QUESTIONNAIRE

Now is the time to use your answers to the body questionnaire you filled in earlier (see pages 32–36). Look back again at each question and try to decide why you ticked the box you chose. You may discover that you find you have agreed with some seemingly opposing statements – for instance, you could have agreed with both 'I am proud of my ethnic background' and 'I dislike the way that people respond to my ethnicity'. It is entirely possible to agree with both these as one statement is concerned with your inner self – how you feel about yourself – but the other is concerned with the response of others to your colour or cultural background. It is also possible to agree that you treat your body with respect, but wish it was different in some way.

Look first at your 'strongly agree' column. Try to decide if there are any themes that unite your strength of feeling. For instance, you may discover that you feel unhappy about your body but do not eat healthily or take exercise. Alternatively, you may discover that you feel all right about your body but sometimes meet people who respond in an unhelpful manner (this, sadly, often happens to people with a disability, and is much more a reflection of the poor education and unhelpful attitudes of society than anything to do with the person with a disability). If you have ticked this column it means you had a powerful emotional response – this could be the mood you are in today or something that is longer term. Relate counsellors often notice that this kind of strong emotion in response to a question can point to a deep concern, and probably one that has been bubbling under the surface for a long time. So reflect on why you felt strongly. This is also true for the 'strongly disagree' column. In fact, any strong response is worth thinking through. This is not to suggest that strong feelings should be avoided. In fact, the world would be a greyer place without them, but you may feel that they demonstrate a need to change some part of your response to your body.

Now look at the middle two columns – 'agree' and 'do not agree'. These columns probably reflect how you feel about your body the majority of the time. The statements for which you ticked these columns are very likely to reflect your conscious feelings about your body. It is also possible that the two columns are interchangeable. For instance, your response to 'I treat my body with respect' could change according to whether you spent last night drinking lager and eating large amounts of curry before staggering home, or have just eaten a virtuous green salad after a jog! Read each question carefully. Agreeing that you 'feel constrained in sexual relationships. . .' is very different from agreeing that you 'try to eat healthily. . .'. As you look back at all the columns, note the questions referring to each section on the following pages and decide what your answers mean to you.

THE BODY IN QUESTION

Having reflected on your body questionnaire, and noted your emotional response to various statements, what do you think about your body now, today? Have you accepted it as it is or do you long for it the way it was five, 10, 20 years ago? Or do you want a body that is very different from how it is today?

Relate counsellors often meet individuals and couples who are out of touch with how they feel about themselves physically. They may be living in the hope that their body will magically return to its old vigour, or have put their life on hold until their body is exactly the right size, weight, etc. To borrow a famous phrase from the group Oasis, the ability to 'be here now' is often more difficult than we imagine. Our attitudes to our physical selves are usually a rich mixture of old memories, current desires, the influence of fashion and our hopes and dreams. You may also have become used to criticising your body for what you perceive to be its weaknesses. Or you may have a partner who criticises the way you look. Whatever the reason, if you feel out of touch with how your body is today, try the following exercise.

YOUR BODY – GETTING IN TOUCH

Exercise One

Find a space where you can lie full length on your back in comfort. If this is not possible for you, find a position that is comfortable and allows you to feel reasonably relaxed. Try not to tense your muscles but breath deeply and evenly. Close your eyes.

Now start a mental journey. Start at your feet. Try to feel the shape of your feet and toes. Follow the shape with your mind and hold the image of your toes – long, short, clean or dirty and so on. Pretend you are drawing your feet in detail. Try to do this without opening your eyes to peek at the real thing! Just use a mental image.

Now do the same thing with each section of your body. Move up the legs to ankle, shin, thigh and bottom, groin and genitals, stomach and chest/breasts, neck, shoulders, arms and hands. Lastly, think about your head and face. Once you have drawn this mental image of the different parts of your body, put it all together. Imagine you are looking at yourself in a mirror.

As you do this, think about the images that probably came crowding in as you undertook the exercise. You may have found yourself remembering unflattering comments about some part of your body, or skipped certain areas because you do not like them. You might also have thought about the areas that you really like – your hairstyle, shapely legs or strong arms. Where do all these emotions and thoughts come from? And are they relevant to how you really are today? For instance, you may have been teased as a child because you were under or overweight. Many people carry this kind of negative self-imagery with them when it is simply no longer relevant. Even if you are still skinny or plump, need this be a source of self-criticism? Imagine all those negative images of yourself being packed in a bag. Now decide what you will do with it – throw it away, shelve it or put it well out of sight. Once you have done this, think about the parts of your body you like. Imagine yourself unpacking these and hanging them in a wardrobe. This may sound a little strange, but I am asking you to honour your body in a way that you may not have done so before. Regarding yourself as worthy of admiration and care is essential for nurturing a healthy attitude to your body. If you can put aside the old 'baggage' of negative images about your body, your remaining positive feelings can influence your attitude to the whole of your body.

Once you have undertaken this imaginary journey, try to practise it a couple of times a week for two or three weeks. You may find you have to struggle with negative feelings and thoughts that return as you attempt to see yourself in a positive light. Try not to worry too much about these as it will take a while to move away from a negative view to a positive one. After all, the views you have of yourself have been formed over several years and will take time to change. You could also try this positive mental imagery for particular parts of your body that you feel especially unhappy about. Concentrate on this area, seeing it as good and part of the real you, rather than a separate part that must be despised.

Finish the exercise by stretching and opening your eyes. Allow yourself a few moments to 'return' to the room and get up. You may wish to write down any of your experiences to reflect on later, but this is not obligatory.

A comment on the desire to alter the body

A hatred of a certain part of themselves often leads people (usually women) to embark on cosmetic surgery. Focusing on one particular body part may be symptomatic of a desire to resolve larger questions about who and what they are. Some people who have cosmetic plastic surgery report that the surgery is satisfying at first, but then they begin to feel dissatisfied with other body parts, and so it goes on.

For other people, who undertake cosmetic surgery because of a disfiguring scar, or after an accident, it can be a liberating experience, enabling the person to feel confident and able to face life again. Even some simple procedures, such as having ears pinned back, can help people to feel better about themselves. But if the desire to change is linked to wider feelings about being unacceptable, or even self-hatred, then it may not be the body part that is at fault, but the mental attitude of the person concerned (see page 116).

Exercise Two

Now that you have completed exercise one, try this exercise. Remove your clothes and look at yourself in a mirror. Allow yourself to feel relaxed and breathe slowly and evenly.

Start by looking at your feet and ankles and gradually work up your body. Instead of allowing negative thoughts and feelings to intrude, concentrate on positive thoughts. Look for the softness of your skin and the curve of your hips, or the strength of your arms or chest, for example. Put aside the negative thoughts that may enter your mind – especially those that relate to your age and size. Concentrate on where you are today – 'be here now' – and think about all that your body does for you each day, even if this has changed over the years.

As you undertake this looking exercise, look at all sides of you. Use another hand mirror to look at your back. If you begin to feel that your body is not as you would wish it to be, use terms that are positive rather than negative. For example, 'my stomach is larger than it used to be, but this is partly because I have been pregnant', or 'I am not as slender as my friend at college, but I am an attractive young woman with a fit body'. A man might use similar ways of looking – for instance, he might tell himself 'I do not have the six pack of the men on magazine covers, but I feel OK about my chest', or 'I have a large appendix scar, but it does not affect my body function'.

When you have finished, put your clothes on and reflect on what you have seen. Most people who undertake this kind of exercise are surprised at how positive they feel about the way they look. If you can allow positive feelings to stay in your mind, you will allow some of the fog of negativity that assails most people when they think about their body, to blow away. If you have found it disturbing, think about why. Perhaps you found it hard to fight off feelings that your body was not up to scratch or became depressed at what you saw. Do not just accept these feelings. Think about where they are coming from. Are they remnants of criticisms that originated years ago? Are they linked to unhelpful attitudes from others? Make a special effort to see yourself through your own eyes, not the eyes of everyone else who has an opinion!

Here is a list of the kind of things that people may have said over the years, with some possible explanations.

Remark	Explanation
'I don't want to play with you because you are too fat/have eczema/wheeze when you run/ can't play football', etc.	Children really can be cruel. This kind of remark can wound and often begins when children are aged about seven or eight. At this age, children begin to make judgements about others based on a desire to belong and feel popular. Children also parrot parental prejudice, so you may have been on the receiving end of an adult bigot by proxy. Unfortunately, this kind of remark can stick in the memory, blighting future feelings about the body. As you read this, allow yourself to put this kind of memory in your baggage and throw it away.

Remark	Explanation
'You are a big girl/boy' or, 'You're a little skinny thing'.	This kind of remark is often linked to a spurious idea of what is 'normal'. Or the speaker may believe that children like teasing of this kind. Either way, the problem lies with them, not you.
'Isn't it a shame you have to wear glasses. You could be so attractive without them'. (Could include any aid to daily life, such as a hearing aid, crutch, etc.)	This is about being 'perfect', and is also about power. It is an attempt to feel superior and to bolster personal self-esteem at the expense of the 'victim'.
'I'm not dancing with you, you are too fat/thin/short/tall/spotty', etc.	This is usually encountered in the teenage years and stems from the intense desire of most teenagers to belong to a group in which they feel accepted. Groups tend to make up their own arbitrary rules and you can be sure that at least one of these 'rules' will exclude you from the 'in-group' at some time. The most important lesson to learn here is that the 'rules' are not real, just part of the tortuous process of growing up.
'I want a blonde/ brunette/ redheaded/slim/ full-figured girlfriend' or 'I want a muscly/ long-haired/ blond/slim/big boyfriend'.	If you are a woman, statements like this could have launched you on a thousand hair-colouring and diet projects! If you are a man, you could have been racing to the gym before the sentence was finished! This kind of remark can cause you to feel a) that you are not good enough as you are and b) that the right way to see yourself is through another's eyes. This is obviously no way to gain body esteem. The chances are that the speaker is fantasising about his or her own self-image, or do they want a fantasy partner who will wave a magic wand, giving *them* the strong self-esteem they desire?

Remark	Explanation
'You have become fatter/older/saggier/ wrinkly – everything's gone south'.	In the West we worship youth. We pretend to ourselves that we will never grow older and our bodies won't age. This can mean that we criticise ourselves and suffer criticisms from partners for perfectly natural changes as we age. Comments of this kind may be less a judgement of you and more an expression of anxiety from the person speaking to you. In fact, they may be voicing their own anxieties about growing older by rudely remarking on how you look.

It is important to understand the root of negative thinking about your body. Much of how you think about yourself today stems from the past. Here are some ideas to help you to overcome these feelings:

- List all the things your body can do for you today. Even if these are limited compared with years or months ago, celebrate the things you can do. For instance, Tanya listed items such as 'walk, talk, be fertile, sing, swim and drive a car'. None of these are especially novel, but are still worth feeling good about.
- Give yourself a compliment about each part of your body. Start with your feet and work upwards. For instance, tell yourself what lovely toe-nails you have, what strong calves, what lean torso, etc. This might sound a little crazy, but it is a personal exercise (no one needs to know what you are thinking) and will help you to feel positive about your body. If it makes you smile, it's worth doing for that alone!
- Imagine you are a statue on a plinth being admired by a crowd of onlookers. Imagine each one praising a different aspect of your form.

- Describe your body to yourself in glowing terms. Use the same kind of language that can be found in adverts in every magazine. Talk about shiny hair, glowing skin, powerful muscles and so on. Do this even if you do not feel confident that it really describes you. Remember, you are countering years of negative thinking that is even more false.

Positive thinking can really make a difference to how you see yourself. Now try the next and last exercise to boost your body esteem.

Exercise Three

Now that you have used your imagination to trace your body and spent time looking at your body as it is today, it is time to move on to an exercise about touch. The most important thing about your body is that it is covered in skin. This is the largest organ in the body and the main source of tactile contact with the world. It is easy to forget how lovely stroking and caressing the skin can be. This is especially true if you feel ashamed of your body and seek to prevent others from touching it. This kind of thinking can also cause you to stop enjoying sensory pleasures. For example, Olive felt that her breasts were too small. Every time her husband, Tom, caressed her breasts, Olive 'screened out' the sensations because she was overcome by anxiety. Her feelings about her breasts, plus her concern that her husband would dislike them, prevented her from understanding a simple truth – whether her breasts were large or small, she could still enjoy his caresses.

The best place to carry out this exercise is in the bath

or shower. You could also enjoy the exercise without bathing, but the warm water can add an extra level of sensuous enjoyment.

1   Choose a time when you can relax and take a bath or shower that can last about half an hour. Undress slowly and get into/under the water. The water should be pleasantly warm rather than hot.

2   Once you are comfortable, use bath oil, gel or body wash to cover your body. If you are using something that creates a lather, you may like to get a good lather going using a sponge (or similar). Ensure you are covered in whatever you have chosen. The object of this exercise is not to get you clean (hopefully there will be other times for this!) but to allow you to feel good about your body, so do not go through a 'washing' ritual that could put you off enjoying the touching for its own sake.

3   Now put the sponge to one side and use your hands to stroke and massage your body. Notice the texture of your skin – smooth or rough, shaved or hairy, taut or loose. Put aside critical feelings about yourself. Just stay with the sensations. Explore areas that you do not touch very much, such as the back of the knees, the elbows, the inside of the thighs and small of the back. Use your hand flat with the fingers spread out, the back of your fingers to give a gentle touch or grip parts of your body firmly. The key point here is to enjoy the touching. Imagine you are 'meeting' your body for the first time and learning how good you are to touch. This exercise is not intended to be specifically sexually arousing, but you may notice you do feel aroused. If this happens, try not to go on

to masturbate as this may detract from your total body experience.

4 Once you have finished touching and enjoying your body, get out of the bath or shower and towel yourself dry. Try to make this part of your touch exercise by taking special care to dry each part of your body.

5 Now find a warm place to lie down and relax for about 15 minutes. You may like to cover yourself with a towel or blanket. Spend this time reflecting on how you felt as you touched yourself. Think about what felt good and why. If you experienced negative thoughts about any part of your body, ask yourself where these thoughts originated from. Many negative thoughts come from old 'messages' given to us from the past that are simply no longer appropriate.

Case Study

Dawn found that her touching exercise was very good as she was able to appreciate her body in a new way, but she ran into problems as she stroked her thighs. She found it very hard to feel happy about touching herself on her thighs and realised that she usually only gave them a perfunctory rub with the shower gel when she washed. After the shower, and while she relaxed, she thought back to where these feelings came from. She found herself remembering being teased at secondary school when she was about 12. A class mate had teased her throughout the year, picking on various aspects of Dawn's physical shape, eventually settling on her thighs which she christened 'thunder thighs'. Dawn had spent many unhappy hours weeping in her room over the teasing but was too embarrassed to tell her parents. Eventually the girl moved away and Dawn felt much happier at school. But she realised that the rude remarks made about her body by the bully had left a mark on her. At the age of 30, the long-term impact of the bullying had stopped her from feeling confident about her legs. She resolved to let go of the feelings that came from the teasing and try to learn to love herself as she was now.

It can be helpful to repeat this exercise a few times, allowing yourself to feel more positive about your body each time you do it. You can vary the exercise by using a good quality massage oil outside the bath. Make sure the room is warm room with soft lighting so that you feel relaxed and comfortable as you caress yourself. You can also play soft music or light a scented oil burner/candle to help you to feel positive about the exercise.

Try telling yourself the following as you stroke your body:

- I like the sensation of stroking the skin on my (name body part)
- I enjoy feeling the weight of my breasts/the shape of my arms/the smoothness of my face. . . (pick any part you like touching to compliment)
- I feel relaxed and at ease
- I want to enjoy my body
- I no longer have to believe teasing or criticisms from the past
- I no longer want to criticise my own body

This kind of 'body positive' attitude can grow from following the exercises outlined above. The next section will look at the impact of change on our view of, and ability to value, our bodies.

THE CHANGING BODY

There is one thing we can all bank on in life and that is that our body will change – and is in fact changing every day. Just as we grow from children to adults, so the progression of the years of adulthood affects our bodies. For some people this is a very gradual process. For others, surgical operations, accidents, childbirth, illness or cosmetic surgery will change the body radically in short time spans. Coming to terms with these changes can be difficult. Relate counsellors often help couples who have faced a body-changing event to integrate resultant feelings and behaviour into their loving relationship.

Case Study

Joanna came to see a Relate counsellor after her mastectomy operation. Joanna had developed breast cancer a year before and had her right breast and some lymph nodes removed. She had been through a terrible time and found it very hard to accept the huge change to her body. Her husband, Frank, loved Joanna, was incredibly relieved that she was still alive, and very much wanted to go on touching and cuddling Joanna as he had done in the past, but Joanna thought he must hate her scarred chest as much as she did and so avoided any physical contact, including sex. As the counselling sessions progressed, Joanna, Frank and the counsellor worked hard on Joanna's perception of her body. This was a long, slow process and Joanna shed many tears of grief at the loss of her breast and the change in her body. Gradually, she was

*able to feel more positive about herself and allowed Frank
to touch her.*

This kind of body change often produces a number of
emotions. Often they follow a pattern, but they can also
occur in a random manner. Here are some of the most
common:

- *Numbness and shock.* Many people who experience
  radical body changes go through a period of dis-
  association at first. Some report feeling as if their body
  belongs to another person, or as if they are watching
  themselves in a mirror. This can be disconcerting and
  confusing, but may act as a protection to the individual's emotions at the start of a phase of adjustment to
  the change.

- *Anger and irritability.* It is common to experience feelings of anger after an operation or illness that changes
  your body. You may feel angry with anyone who is
  connected to the body change you have endured. For
  instance, doctors and nurses often have to deal with
  patients venting their anger after a surgical procedure.
  Patients may shout at a surgeon who has saved their
  life but had to alter their body to achieve this.
  Alternatively, they may become angry with a partner
  for some perceived lack of support, with children for
  not understanding how they feel or with the world in
  general for the changed circumstances they find themselves in. This kind of anger is often not related to the
  recipient at all – they just happen to get in the way of
  strong feelings! It is also natural and important to
  allow yourself to feel the anger and to recognise that
  this is a natural part of coping with the change. You

may feel angry with others, but the anger really comes from your personal grief and sadness at the loss of what you thought was 'you', together with the need to deal with and make sense of the change.

- *Sadness and despair.* These feelings can accompany and spark off feelings of anger or alternate with feelings of irritability, so that you feel as if you are on an emotional roller coaster. All of this can affect how you feel about your body and how you relate to others. Crying or wanting to cut yourself off from friends and family are all symptoms of this stage. As with anger, it is important to understand that these are natural responses to a tough time. It is generally better to allow yourself to weep than to crush the desire to express your unhappiness as repressing these powerful emotions can cause more problems. Use the support of friends or get professional help to see you through this phase.
- *Longing and yearning.* You may find yourself longing for the clock to be turned back or for everything to be different. Some people dream of being how they were before their operation, for instance. You may also feel as if you are stuck in a rut, unable to move forward into a new lifestyle because you want your body to be the way it was before. This can have the effect of immobilising you, both physically and emotionally. Some physiotherapists report that helping people to recover after a body-changing event can be difficult if the yearning phase is protracted. The patient may simply not want to face the reality of the change to their body and therefore not engage with any treatment to address the problem. This is understandable,

but can be difficult for friends and family to understand. They may seem impatient for you to grasp the
future or push you to accept treatment you feel uncertain you are ready for.

Here are some practical ideas to help you to cope with
body change:

Numbness and shock

- Allow yourself time to register what has happened to
  you. Avoid making snap decisions over anything.
- Think through what has happened to you. See it like a
  film in your head, and watch the scenes. As you do
  this, notice the emotions you felt at the time and allow
  yourself to feel these.
- Tell other people the 'story' of what happened to you.
  You may fear boring everybody but it is important for
  you to do this in order to get a grip on what happened
  and what it meant to you.

Anger and irritability

- Think through who or what you are really angry with.
  You may want to blame the surgeon or other driver
  who ran into your car, but at least some of your rage
  may be directed at your changed situation. Of course,
  this is not to suggest that you should not seek recom-
  pense for a bungled operation or an accident caused
  through the careless driving of another.
- Write down all your angry feelings and thoughts.
  Head your paper 'I am angry because . . .'. This can be
  extremely cathartic. You may like to do something

symbolic with the sheet of paper such as burning it or tearing it into lots of little pieces. However, do not send it to whoever you hold responsible for what has happened – this will only make things worse. Use it as an outlet for your anger rather than a score sheet to be held against another.

- Choose a time when you are alone, pile the bed with pillows and hit them with a rolled up newspaper or magazine. This allows your anger to be discharged safely.
- If possible, take gentle exercise. Walking, swimming or dancing can all help you to feel more relaxed and less tense. If you are able, more vigorous exercise, such as team sports or running, can also be helpful.

Sadness and despair

- Talk to people you trust about your feelings. Do not be afraid to show your sadness. You may not weep, but this does not mean you do not feel sad. Try to find the words to express your emotions.
- Keep a diary. Writing or taping a diary can allow you to express your feelings each day. You may begin to notice that a pattern emerges or that you are gradually making sense of what happened to you, and this can be encouraging. Some research on arthritis sufferers has found that those who keep a regular journal feel they tolerate their pain more successfully. Creative writing is also good as this can help you to let go of sadness. Poems, stories, plays – anything in this mode is useful. You may never want another person to read them, but the aim is to allow *you* to understand *your* feelings.

- Paint or draw your feelings. It does not matter if you have only ever attempted stick men before, drawing how you see your body now, or your feelings in swirls of colour, can really make a difference. (Art therapists specialise in this – you may find an art therapist in your area.)
- Seek professional help. Talking to a counsellor can help you to deal with change. Some hospitals offer sessions with specialist counsellors in the area of body change you are experiencing (cancer, for instance) or look for a self-help group on the particular problem you have. (Your GP should be able to point you towards an appropriate contact.)

Longing and yearning

- Make a list of all the things you *can* do. They may be different from what you could do before the change you have experienced, but could they be interesting and satisfying in a different way?
- Revisit places and people who have a link to the past. This may seem a strange thing to suggest, but sometimes confronting reminders of the past in a tangible way can exorcise the feeling that the past is more attractive than the present. Take a friend with you if you want extra support. For instance, you might try visiting the hospital where you were operated on or the house you lived in before an illness. Just sitting in the car outside the place can help you to face the longing and allow you to move on to an acceptance of where you are today – even if this is emotionally and/or physically painful.

- Think about the specifics of what you are yearning for. Instead of saying 'I wish everything could be the way it was' say, 'I wish I could walk to the corner shop to buy my paper the way I used to' (or whatever is right for you). Once you have done this, you can think about a way to achieve what you have lost. Maybe you cannot physically walk to the shop, but could you have the paper delivered? Or take a short walk, perhaps just a few hundred yards, round the block? Or read the paper on the Internet? Look for ways to resolve the longing rather than feel you cannot change anything.

A changed body is sometimes caused by a traumatic event – an accident, an operation or some other problem – or simply by the process of time. If you are alive, this is an inevitable truth! If you are young, it may seem unimaginable that you will one day feel less mobile or have a wrinkled face. But this is how it will be. In the film *Shirley Valentine*, Shirley's Greek lover tells her, 'Do not hide your stretch marks – they are beautiful and a sign of the life you carried'. Shirley makes a rude reply, but perhaps he is right – we should all be proud of the signs of life we have etched on our faces and bodies instead of trying to hide them.

MAINTAINING A HEALTHY BODY

Maintaining a healthy body has been widely discussed in recent years. Society is feeling the effects of unhealthy past lifestyles with more and more people suffering from heart disease (heart disease is currently responsible for more deaths than any other disease in the UK), lung cancers and obesity. As a nation we are eating more refined foods and taking less exercise. This can have a detrimental effect on our health. Here are some basic steps towards maintaining a healthy lifestyle. If you want to know more, ask your GP or practice nurse for information about diet, nutrition, exercise and other ways to improve your lifestyle.

Diet

There are four main groups of foods:

Proteins – found in meat, beans and pulses, fish, dairy products and cereals.

Carbohydrates – found in cereals, grains and root vegetables.

Fats – found in animal products, dairy products and eggs. Also found in fish, corn oil, poultry and other products such as olives.

Fibre – found mainly in plant products.

For a healthy diet, you need to eat food from all of these groups. However, the daily amount needed from each group varies.

Fats – keep these to a minimum. Eat low-fat yoghurts, cheese and skimmed or semi-skimmed milk. Watch out for hidden fats in crisps, cakes, biscuits and other products that sometimes claim to be 'lower fat'. The recommended maximum amount of fat for a woman per day is 70g in 2000 calories. For a man it is 95g in 2500 calories. Avoid frying food and use the grill instead.

Carbohydrates – try to eat brown bread, unrefined cereals, brown rice and pasta as these contain fibre and other nutrients that are often not present in 'white', refined alternatives. Potatoes contain carbohydrate, but should be eaten in their 'jacket' for maximum health benefit. Frying and boiling remove vital nutrients, as well as adding calories in the form of fat (as in chips).

Protein – choose fish, chicken and turkey rather than their high-fat alternatives such as red meat. Beans contain first-class protein so a vegetarian diet should contain plenty of beans, lentils and other pulses as well as vegetables.

Fibre – all fruit and vegetables contain fibre. The most recent healthy eating advice is to eat five portions of fresh fruit and vegetables every day. You may wish to replace one portion of fruit with a glass of fruit juice or eat frozen fruit and vegetables, but fibre in any form has been proven to prevent bowel cancer and improves digestion. You can also obtain fibre from some cereals – weetabix, for example – but avoid sugary cereals as these often do not contain as much fibre and are bad for teeth and weight maintenance.

Exercise

Exercise can improve muscle tone, help you to sleep better and aid concentration. As a nation of so-called 'couch potatoes' there is no doubt that we could probably all do with more exercise! People are often put off by the idea that exercise means rushing to the gym to lift weights. In reality, regular, fairly short periods of exercise are better for you than hours spent exercising one week, followed by no exercise for a month. Approximately three 20-minute sessions a week are ideal, or a little exercise each day, perhaps of shorter duration. Here are some suggestions to increase your daily exercise quota:

- Use stairs instead of lifts
- Take up walking for pleasure – enjoy country rambles or strolls around the city
- Swim regularly. Many pools now have 'aquarobic' classes. This can help you to exercise without feeling too hot and bothered as the water keeps you cool
- Take up, or resume, a sport you would or may enjoy. You do not have to play competitively, just for fun
- Go dancing! You may not want to go to the local night-club, but you could join a line dancing or salsa class
- Buy an exercise video and promise yourself you will do it three times a week

Lifestyle

Many people's lifestyles are bad for their health. Smoking, drinking and drug misuse can lead to ill health and many other difficulties. If you are a long-time smoker or drinker, you probably know the risks. Self-motivation is crucial to change this kind of behaviour. If you want specific help on dealing with these issues, check out the helping agencies in your local *Yellow Pages*. However, here are some ways of thinking about changing unhealthy lifestyles:

- Think about how the issue affects you at a personal level. For instance, if you stopped smoking you could have a lot more disposable income for other, less damaging, pleasures.
- Choose something that would motivate you to make the change. For example, you may decide to cut down your alcohol consumption so you can spend more time with your children.
- Look for the trigger to your habit. Do you tend to drink/smoke/take drugs to avoid stress and anxiety? Could you seek alternative ways of dealing with this?
- Consider how your behaviour affects the people you care about. Try to use this insight as a help towards change. For example, you may feel relaxed after smoking dope, but it may mean you are emotionally distanced from your partner.

IN CONCLUSION

Who we are is presented to the world through our bodies. For some people, this is a source of difficulty and can undermine personal self-esteem. But much of our anxiety about bodily self-esteem comes from peer-group pressure, media images of fashionable bodies and self-criticism. We can allow ourselves to feel good about our bodies by challenging negative views of our bodies. These are often the result of unhappy past experiences and can be re-evaluated. We can also seek to maintain healthy bodies by eating well, exercising regularly and stopping or cutting down on habits that undermine our health.

Chapter 4

EMOTIONAL SELF-ESTEEM – HOW TO FEEL AT EASE WITH EMOTION

We experience emotion every day. You may know that you are the kind of person who is aware of emotion and its effect on your life. Or you may not be very aware of emotion, remaining relatively untouched by the storms of feelings that others report. Emotions can create ecstasy, make us cry or cause us to behave in a manner that seems completely out of character. If we were all like Mr Spock, the TV character who suppressed or did not recognise his feelings from the sci-fi series *Star Trek*, we would live very dull lives. Emotion can take us to the heights of pleasure and the depths of misery. This is not only true for relationships, but also for our experience of music, films, books and so on. Not all of us wish to wear our hearts on our sleeves, but understanding emotion, as well as feeling comfortable with expressing emotion, can enable us to have a positive sense of self-esteem.

SELF-ESTEEM AND EMOTION

It might be argued that as emotion is uncontrollable you just have to 'roll with it' in order to have a reasonably comfortable existence. To some extent this is true. We do have to experience emotion in an immediate way – we cannot plan to feel happy or sad on a certain day and at a certain time. But we can expect to feel particular emotions at certain events – the mother who weeps at her daughter's wedding or the man who feels hurt because his partner has forgotten his birthday – are recognisable. We know that some emotions are likely given a particular set of events. It is when our emotions are either unknown to us or overwhelm us that self-esteem can be affected. Here are some common concerns that people describe to Relate counsellors.

COMMON PROBLEMS

1 You feel unable to access your feelings. Some people describe this as feeling 'numb'. They may observe events or interact with others where emotion might be expected to be felt, but feel very little. For example, Tim often missed the point of emotional scenes in films because he could not identify with what was happening.

2 You are bathed in a sea of emotionality. Every small thing that happens sets off a stream of emotion that causes you to feel confused and hyped up. This can lead to an upward spiral of anxiety that makes you feel afraid of any event that causes emotion. For

example, Jill was often described as a 'drama queen' by her friends as she could become highly emotional in almost any situation.

3 You tend to react to certain situations with a particular emotion. For instance, Lucas knew that any criticism of his family tended to put him in a rage. He was unable to explain, to himself or others, what sparked this strong response.

4 You find you respond to most situations that demand an emotional response with anger, tears, depression and withdrawal. For example, Sharon found it very hard to stand her ground with her bullying boss because she always began to weep if challenged.

As you have already filled in your Emotional Self questionnaire you may find that you have identified one or more of the above scenarios for yourself. Your questionnaire may have shown you that you are comfortable with emotion, able to respond to, or demonstrate, appropriate emotion in all your relationships. Or you could have found that emotion is hard to handle, sometimes allowing your feelings to sweep you away, or hardly feel a thing when you think you should. The common problems listed above are all detrimental to positive self-esteem. Here are some case studies that match the concerns mentioned above. All of them demonstrate how difficulties with emotion can lead to a lowered self-esteem.

Case Study

Marsha was often described by her friends as 'cool' or 'focused'. She seemed able to take decisions even when everyone around her was panicking. It was this quality that made her an excellent A&E nurse. Marsha could take tough decisions when faced with a medical emergency, and did not seem to suffer the emotional responses of her colleagues after particularly traumatic situations. However, during her routine appraisal her manager told her that she was often perceived as uncaring and brusque towards the relatives of the patients she treated. They often reported that she delivered bad news as if she was a robot, or in a manner that left them feeling uncertain about what was really happening. Her colleagues also felt that she was difficult to know as part of the team, and often excluded her from parties or social events. Marsha realised that the appraisal had pinpointed something about her that was hard to admit to. She knew she was a good nurse, but felt a lowering of self-esteem when colleagues were sought out by relatives, even when she had undertaken most of the treatment.

This kind of inability to empathise with the emotions that others are going through can lead to a feeling of isolation and loneliness. In extreme cases it can lead to a particular syndrome called Asperger's Syndrome. This genetic syndrome causes individuals to seem unable to recognise distress or pleasure in others. Sufferers may fail to respond as their partner or friends would wish. This syndrome appears to relate to autism at some levels, but more research in this area is needed to improve understanding. More commonly, many people who appear unemotional are actually repressing strong feelings through anxiety. For some, this may be because they were taught not to be emotional as a child. Perhaps a parent told them 'not to make a fuss' if they hurt them-selves or did well at school. This can lead to children learning that emotions are not acceptable in public. If this sounds like you, and you would like to be more aware of your feelings, try the following ideas:

- Keep an emotion journal. Write down what happens to you and any emotions you associate with your day. At first, you may not find this easy, but gradually your feelings and thoughts will come to the surface.

- In social situations, observe how others are behaving. If everyone else seems sad or happy, think about why this is so.

- Use your imagination. If others tell you that you 'have missed the point' or that you appear unsympathetic, try to imagine what it would be like to be them. See yourself feeling what they feel. For instance, Marsha tried this technique when telling a parent that their child was seriously ill. She found it much easier once she had entered into the emotional world of the parent, and this helped her to feel better about her work.

- Get out of the habit of repressing feeling. Feeling can sometimes be almost physical – knots in the stomach, a feeling of lightness, pleasure. Take notice of these, however fleeting. You may fear being overwhelmed with pain or joy, but try not to be afraid. In most people there are natural inhibitions that prevent them from looking foolish in public. This is not to say that a good cry isn't sometimes very good for you!

- Try putting yourself in a situation where you are likely to experience strong emotion – such as a dare-devil roller-coaster ride or a moving musical concert. Watch yourself for the sparks of feeling that rise to the surface. If you are like Marsha, you may immediately stamp on these in order to appear calm. But these are both situations where you are expected to feel very excited or emotional, so let go instead of restraining yourself.

The benefit of being aware of your feelings is that you are less likely to feel isolated from others and will be able to make sense of what is going on around you in a much better way. You will also gain in self-esteem as others see you as more sensitive and caring.

Case Study

Georgina was married with two small children when her husband told her he thought he could not cope with being married to her any more. Georgina was stunned when he explained he could not cope with her extreme emotional highs and lows. Georgina knew that she was prone to highly emotional responses to daily events, but felt that this was a family trait as her mother was just the same. Everyone in the family tiptoed around her mother because of her 'nerves' and were extremely anxious to avoid any kind of upset. Georgina could get wound up over anything. She would shout and yell about not being able to find a clean blouse for her daughter, and the next minute would be hugging and kissing her husband because he had cooked the breakfast for her. She lived on her feelings, but did not realise what this did to her husband and daughters. They often felt they did not know how to react to events, and sometimes watched Georgina to see what mood she was in before taking any action, or even speaking. Despite the fact that Georgina's emotions were so near the surface, she often felt confused about how she really did feel and was sometimes depressed and miserable. Her ups and downs left her feeling mentally exhausted and close to tears instead of in touch with her feelings.

Georgina's emotional behaviour is the equivalent of being tossed around on a stormy sea. The emotional waves that engulf people who 'feel everything' actually prevent them from understanding what is happening to them. Instead they may feel as if they are drowning and unable to relate to those around them because they are concentrating on staying afloat rather than tuning in to family or friends when they need to. This kind of self-absorption can be a problem in friendships because it may seem to the friend that everything is one way, rather than a shared, support- ive relationship where there is equal room for both people to express their thoughts and feelings. If you recognise yourself in this case study, try the following:

- Before you express your emotions, listen and watch the people around you. Try to guess what they want or need.
- Ask yourself what level of feeling is suitable for the event you are dealing with. For instance, is it really necessary to make a huge fuss over a lost hairbrush? Could you handle the situation better without the over- reaction?
- Ask someone you trust to help you to pitch your emo- tional level appropriately for the situation. Ask them to say something like, 'It's OK' or, 'Less emotion would be OK here'. Make sure this is done in a caring and affectionate way, not as a put-down, or it could make things much worse.

• Try to work out why you use emotion in the way that you do. Could it be a smoke screen, preventing you from looking at what is really going on? It is possible that this kind of heightened feeling is a psychological preventative measure to stop you learning about what is going on around you, or to shield you from real hurt. If you can understand this it can have the effect of improving your emotional sensibilities. Relate counselling can be helpful in this scenario.

Case Study

Mike was a lecturer at a local community college and was perceived by his students to be a good teacher. He was able to communicate well and often worked long hours to ensure their success in exams. However, Mike was also well known for his temper, although his students never saw this side of his character. To his colleagues and family, Mike's outbursts were erratic and unpredictable. But they did have a thread of continuity. Mike was extremely sensitive about his professional qualifications and background. He had left school early and achieved all his qualifications through extremely hard work at night school. Mike often told himself that his colleagues had had it all 'too easy' and did not know the meaning of 'hard work'. Consequently, it only took one mention of another colleague's success, or for his wife to point out how well a friend was doing in their career, for Mike to go off the deep end. He often shouted and was well known for storming out. Often his colleagues and family would be mystified as to what had caused his outburst. Mike usually calmed down quickly, but his anger often left others fearful of his response to simple conversations.

Mike's emotions were generally well balanced, but he had a 'sore spot' that could lead to extreme responses. This kind of emotional response is often the result of lack of self-esteem. Mike felt vulnerable because he perceived his education as sub-standard and thought this was how his colleagues felt. His bluster is really an attempt to cover his vulnerability and to prevent others from probing this part of himself that he feels is somehow not 'good enough'. Often in these situations, the problem area is related to a particular perception of a fault or failing, but the failing is often only seen this way by the person themselves. For instance, Mike's wife was proud of her husband's achievements, especially as he had undertaken so much study entirely through self-motivation. If you recognise yourself in this scenario, here are some ideas to help you to make sense of your response:

• Next time you find yourself sounding off, think about what has sparked this response. It may not always be absolutely clear. For instance, Joan found herself shouting at her daughter when she refused to eat her evening meal. Joan subsequently realised that this was linked to her own problems as a teenager with a mother who insisted she ate everything that was put in front of her. Joan realised that she often found food a problem area, and began to change her approach to cooking and serving meals.
• Ask someone you trust (a partner is ideal) if they can understand why you are upset. They may have spotted your 'sore spot' long ago, but been afraid to talk to you about it.
• Consider whether you have other, less displayed, emotions about a particular issue. If you always shout

or yell, could you also feel tearful or depressed? Identifying these alternate emotions may seem to add to your problems, but it is actually a way of gaining a balanced view of what you feel. Allowing yourself to admit you actually feel miserable or surprised by your emotions is a step towards healing the sensitive areas, allowing you to achieve a healthy balance in your emotional life.

Case Study

Sam was the single father of two sons – Roddy, aged 10, and Oliver, aged 8. Sam's wife had died in a car accident when Oliver was six months old, and he had brought them up on his own. It had often been very hard to manage, especially as Sam tried to hold down a job as well. His parents had been extremely supportive, but his wife's father had often been less than helpful in his dealings with Sam. He often criticised Sam, telling him to behave differently with the boys for instance. He felt that the boys were 'mollycoddled' and needed 'toughening up'. Sam did not agree with him at all, but found he could only respond in one way when his father-in-law put him down. Sam withdrew into himself, becoming silent and unresponsive. This tended to infuriate his father-in-law, causing the situation to escalate into a major incident. Sam knew that he felt angry inside, but could not let his feelings come to the surface. He sought counselling to try to understand why he responded the way he did and, with the help of the counsellor, soon realised that he did the same thing in a variety of settings. He often withdrew if challenged at work, and sometimes pulled back from confrontations with his sons. He also traced the same pattern of behaviour as a child, spending hours alone in his bedroom if his parents raised their voice to him. Sam realised that he retreated into his private world because it felt safe and protected him from unpleasant repercussions. Sam saw that as well as not dealing with anger head-on, he also often felt numb to any other kind of emotion – excitement, pleasant anticipation or joy. Gradually Sam began to allow himself to express his feelings rather than simply pulling back from situations where emotion could or should be expressed.

This kind of response – a kind of emotional 'one-note samba' can come about for a variety of reasons. Sometimes it blocks other feelings that could make you feel vulnerable. For instance, being angry is better than being scared or embarrassed and forms a shell of protection that can be hard to break through. Tears, the use of humour and the avoidance of emotional situations are all common 'one-emotion' responses and could be all too familiar to you. If you recognise yourself, try the following to help you to demonstrate a range of feelings.

• When you are next in an emotional situation, ask yourself what you are really feeling inside. Your usual response may immediately rise to the surface, but are you really feeling panicky, anxious, unsure or wondering what the others involved are feeling?

• Ask yourself what you fear might happen if you reveal your true feelings. For example, Freddie often blustered in situations at work where he felt out of his depth. He was afraid to appear ignorant, so he put his colleagues at arm's length rather than risk appearing foolish. Once you have faced your fear, think about whether there are practical ways to overcome it. Freddie might have asked for extra training support or to shadow a colleague who was familiar with the procedure he felt unsure about.

- Look at the benefits that could follow if you faced the fear. In this situation, it is common for people to see only negative fallout from showing feeling. Kim was afraid to show her feelings because she thought her boyfriend would take flight and avoid committing to her. But when Kim told him how strongly she felt about him, he was delighted that she felt the same as him, and said he had also been afraid to admit to his feelings of love for lack of encouragement!

- Consider where you learnt this kind of emotional response from. If you recognise similar traits in family or friends, ask yourself if they have benefited those who seem to be similar to you. Usually the answer to this kind of question is 'no' because a constant playing on one emotion is crippling. It is rather like a footballer training only one leg to play with. In a game he cannot run or pass the ball to team mates. He cannot score a goal. A single emotional response to any situation can cause you to feel cut off from others and can prevent you from making close relationships.

A balanced emotional life can really help you to feel better about yourself. You will be able to show appropriate feelings at the moment you most need to. Others will know what you think and feel and be able to respond to you in a way that will allow you to communicate and interact with more success.

Now that you have read this section on different styles of emotional responses, try filling in the following table to help you to make sense of your emotions. I have given you a list of some common emotions, but add any others that are most appropriate to you.

My emotion	What I do when I feel this emotion?	What I would like to do?	What would help me to achieve balance in this area?
Fear			
Anxiety			
Happiness			
Excitement			
Anger			

My emotion	What I do when I feel this emotion?	What I would like to do?	What would help me to achieve balance in this area?
Sadness			
Uncertainty			
Embarrassment			
Jealousy			

Fill in the table writing notes in the three columns. In column one, write what happens most often to you. In column two, write anything that you would like to do. For example, you may want to tell your friend that she means the world to you but have never done this because you fear being embarrassed. In column three, write down some practical ideas for achieving your goal. For instance, maybe you cannot tell your friend face to face, but could write a letter, card or e-mail with the same message. As you fill in the columns, look for the benefits of expressing a wide range of emotions, such as less stress and better connections with those around you.

THE ROLE OF DEFENCES IN EMOTIONAL SELF-ESTEEM

Do you think of yourself as defensive? Do others tell you that you are 'prickly'? Or are you open to new ideas and experiences? Whatever your stance, it is certain that you do have some defences. In fact, far from being a bad thing, emotional defences are crucial to our development as human beings. So where do these come from and why do we develop them in the first place?

It has become common in recent years, and especially since counselling and psychotherapy have entered everyday experience, to hear people talk about others as having 'high defences' or 'being very defensive'. This is a way of describing a particular kind of emotional response to a particular situation. In this situation, an individual behaves like a country in constant fear of invasion. The country positions soldiers on its defences and borders and instigates an attack if it feels that the enemy is threatening. A person who is on high emotional defence alert will often see trouble where there is none, and will act (or react) quickly, often in an angry way, in order to repel a perceived emotional attack. This kind of response can be a learned response – that is, one that comes from past experience or achieved its aim on at least one previous occasion. It then becomes a frequently used gambit to prevent challenge or further development of other feelings. But for most people defences are simply part of everyday life. We may not even notice that we have them, and in some specific situations they are needed simply in order to survive.

HOW EMOTIONAL DEFENCES DEVELOP

In babyhood, our emotional and physical needs are there for all to see. If we are hungry, we cry. If we are happy, we gurgle or giggle. If we are frustrated, we lie down on the supermarket floor and kick our legs because mum will not buy us chocolate! As we grow up we learn that this kind of behaviour is not always appropriate. We become socialised – that is, we learn by observing others that laughing when someone hurts themselves or screaming when our lunch is five minutes late is regarded as 'bad' behaviour and sometimes punished. We also receive rewards for behaviour that our relatives want to reinforce – saying thank you for a gift, being willing to share our toys with a brother or sister. Some rewards are tangible – a new bike for doing well at school, for instance. Others are less marked but nevertheless important. We may receive a cuddle when we laugh in response to a game, or be praised for sitting quietly through a church service. Gradually we learn to mask some emotional responses and accentuate others. After all, if you always told your neighbour what you thought of them or burst into tears when you found your favourite video had been loaned to someone else, life would be very difficult. This process is called sublimation or repression and is very important. We often know that someone has a mental illness when this system breaks down. People who have previously behaved in an acceptable way may suddenly begin to attack others verbally, crossing the divide that separates socially acceptable behaviour from unacceptable. Defences help us all to live together in a sociable manner. If we constantly expressed every emotion that flickered through our consciousness, we would be worn out at the end of the average day!

We also need emotional defences for our own protection. Everyone has individual areas that are sensitive to criticism, being ignored or agitated. These are probably unique to each one of us, but there are some themes that you may identify with:

- *Anxiety about being accepted.* Most of us want to be part of a group of like-minded people – whether train spotters, cycling enthusiasts or whatever interests you. The fear of being an outcast and unaccepted is quite deep in human kind, probably because we rely on the support of our group to sustain us, both physically and emotionally. This can be especially true for minority groups in a foreign country. In this situation, special attention is often given to rituals or other group activities to encourage identification. These can form part of group psychological defences, and are often much needed in places where the minority group may feel under threat. So in order to remain accepted we may put aside personal desires. This causes us to build an emotional defence – that is, to prevent others from suspecting we may want to behave or think differently from what is generally accepted as 'normal' in a particular group.

• *Defences against being controlled.* This may seem to conflict with the anxiety about being accepted, but is quite common. It begins to assert itself most strongly in the teenage years, when children begin to develop personal tastes and beliefs. Teenagers are well known for rebelling, experimenting for themselves, and reject- ing everything their parents enjoy or believe in.

• *Concerns about appearing vulnerable.* Many people have a defensive mechanism to stop them appearing vulnerable. Usually this is related to loss of face in some way. For example, we may fear appearing stupid if we cannot answer a question, so we avoid eye contact, sit at the back of the class, or take other evasive action. Many people are also defensive about telling others how much they care for them. This seems to be a peculiarly British trait (and one that does not serve us very well). This kind of defence may come from the notion that a child may be spoiled if you praise him or her, or a secret anxiety that affection is not returned. Vulnerability may serve a purpose if it could cause you to be rejected from a group you wish to belong to. A skewed way of looking at this is to imagine belonging to a group of criminals. To appear to care about robbing strangers of their goods could mean ejection from the group.

• *Defences against danger.* In our primitive state, this kind of defence was important. We used our knowledge and intuition to avoid dangerous areas where perhaps there were wild animals or steep falls. Today we may not face the same kinds of danger, but we still instinctively construct defences against situations that feel emotionally dangerous. We may avoid people we fear or certain careers because we believe they are dangerous. For example, Diana felt she could never train as a teacher because she believed that school violence was on the increase.

Many defences work for us, allowing us to go about our daily lives. For instance, nurses in A&E departments may have to turn on a special kind of defence when dealing with people in extreme situations. Repugnance at dealing with infected wounds or blood is replaced by a professional standard that allows the nurse to do his or her job. This kind of defence is acquired through training, allowing the nurse to carry on when many of us would have given up. Sometimes 'professional defences' are characterised by group identity and special language. The medical community is well known for this, probably because our primitive response to illness is avoidance, and this has to be overcome in order to care for a sick person. A special language and behaviour allow the carer to identify strongly with a professionally supportive community.

But many defences simply distance us from our real

feelings, and can isolate us, causing us to feel less close to others. Some defences also prevent us from taking important decisions about the future. For example, Roger was very anxious about living alone, so he justified his decision to live with his wife, even though he felt very unhappy, by telling himself the marriage would improve the following year, even though this had never happened in previous years.

SPOTTING DEFENCES AT WORK

It is often possible to see defences working all around you in conversations with friends, or even observing passengers on a bus! Watch out for the following next time you are with a group of friends:

- *The use of humour.* Humour can be a classic defence. Laughing at someone else's suggestion around the board table or sniggering in class about a fellow student are defences because they put the other person down, but also deflect attention from the individual's own shortcomings. Some people also use self-deprecating humour (think of Woody Allen) as a defence to avoid exposing their own problems or abilities. It is often true that the 'class clown' is an intelligent person who is afraid to show their mental abilities in case they are teased. Humour can also give a comparatively power-less person some kind of kudos because making other people laugh is valued. You may also meet the kind of person who answers every question with a joke. This is designed to put you off guard and to prevent you from getting to know the real person behind the joke, so disguising a fear of vulnerability.

- *Snapping or sniping*. Putting other people in their place can be a powerful defence system. The aim is to cause the other to retreat and avoid further conversation. Many couples experience this, especially if discussion turns towards a particularly difficult situation. For example, Bill was keen to be seen as a better driver than his sister, Michelle. If Michelle drove the car, with Bill as a passenger, he would continually criticise her driving style. Eventually, Michelle refused to take him in the car and Bill felt he was vindicated.

- *Bluster and anger*. Perhaps the most common defence in action. All the types of behaviour associated with anger – shouting, slamming doors and demanding – can be defensive moves designed to shut down further communication. Closing down further discussion allows a situation to stay as it is. This is a defence against change, and all the difficulties and challenges that change often brings with it. Rose did not want to move house, so every time her boyfriend asked her to move in with him she instigated a huge row. Rose was not aware that she was acting defensively, but just felt anxious and uncomfortable.

- *Withdrawal and closing down*. An extremely common defence that can cause couples and others to feel frustrated at the lack of communication. Jane constantly encountered this problem with her father, George. Jane was worried about her father's frailty and asked him to consider moving into a nursing home. George refused to discuss the matter every time Jane raised it, causing her great anxiety. She realised that George was worried about his loss of independence but was completely prevented from discussing the subject by George's defensive emotional shut down.

- *Attack and control.* Controlling certain situations can be a powerful defence mechanism. This can also be linked to attack, sometimes as an angry outlet, and at other times in a more subtle format. For example, Marianne never agreed to make love when her partner asked her. She would usually find an excuse, but would then ask for sex the next day. Marianne wanted to control their intimate life, although she was not aware of this desire. The root of her need to control came from a previous marriage where her husband had been brutal in his sexual demands. Marianne had felt demeaned and so sought to control sex in her new partnership. Her partner was not happy with the situation, but knew about the previous problem and tolerated her approach. Attack can also take several forms. It may be overt – as when one toddler seizes a toy from another before they can play with it – or in adults less obvious. For instance, it is not unusual for siblings to be jealous of one another, even in adulthood. Sometimes one will race the other to have the first grandchild, get a better job or degree, or even moan about the brother or sister to their parents. In this case, the defence is against the other sibling being seen as better loved and a demand to be number one in their parents' hearts, even in much later life.

- *Blame.* Blaming others for faults or problems is a deflector defence. It is born out of fear of being held responsible and anxiety about the possibility of not being able to put the problem right. Bart Simpson, of

The Simpsons cartoon, is a master at this form of defence. His 'I didn't do it. Nobody saw me. No-one can prove it' is a typical blame response, and is often heard from Homer Simpson as well. Most of us employ blame at some point in life, and in car accidents it has spawned an industry!

WHAT IS YOUR FAVOURED DEFENCE?

Use the grid below to work out what kind of defence you use, and whether it serves a valid purpose in your life.

Usual defence	When used	Why is this form used?	What purpose does it serve?
Humour			
Snapping and sniping			
Bluster			
Anger			
Withdrawal			
Closing down/ shutting out			
Attack			
Control			
Blame			

Use the columns to work out the kind of defences you may operate. Ask yourself why you use the form of defence you do and if it aids your relationships, or gets in the way of everyday interactions.

You might also recognise other defences in yourself. Add these to the table to help you to work out how you respond to emotional situations.

WHY YOU NEED DEFENCES

Everybody needs defences of some kind. To be emotionally naked would be like going back to babyhood. Defences happen naturally as we grow and mature. In themselves they are not harmful or wrong, but when they prevent us from forming loving relationships or getting on with a work colleague, they can blight our lives. The importance of defences is that they allow us to have a 'safe' place to retreat to. If we feel shy, it may be a natural protection that prevents us from having to face a room full of people when we are not ready for it. An extremely common defence is to block out unpleasant events, and even delete them from memory. For example, Kevin had a serious car accident and was badly injured. He did recover, but could recall little of the accident. This enabled him to look to the future rather than the past, and work on recovering his strength. But Kevin had a problem. Months afterwards he was still unable to travel in a car. The trauma had affected him at a deep level so that he became extremely anxious about travelling by car. After a while, he approached a psychologist who helped him to break down his fear and learn to travel in a car again.

DEFEATING UNHELPFUL DEFENCES

Now that you have read about defences, and analysed some of your own personal defences, here are some tips on how to stop using defences that are preventing you from having satisfying relationships in different areas of your life.

Anger

Using anger can sometimes be appropriate, especially if you have something to be justifiably angry about (but not verbal or physical aggression). Storming out often means that no difficult situation is ever fully resolved. Next time you become aware of using anger as a defence, ask yourself what you feel you are defending. Is it lack of confidence? Or an anxiety that someone else is more knowledgeable than you? Talk to the person you are using the defence on and try to develop a relationship that does not depend on your angry defence. Develop the ability to ask for help or support rather than creating a ring of unapproachability around yourself.

Humour

Telling jokes or teasing others is usually a sign of a low sense of self-esteem or a basic fear of not being able to compete on the same level as others. Some humour can create a warm relationship (the late comedian Les Dawson is quoted as saying that 'he laughed women into bed') but often it simply means that trust is hard to develop because the partner of a humorist is never sure what is real and what is a joke. This is how the humour defence works – it puts other people on an unstable emotional platform from where it is hard to develop a relationship. If you tend to make people laugh a lot to avoid talking about feelings, try to switch off your humour for short periods of time. Ask your partner for their response to the new you. You are likely to find that they like someone who is genuine rather than constantly fooling around. This is not to say that a sense of humour is not valued, but it should be used in an appropriate manner to enrich everyday life rather than as a mask to prevent you from having to discuss the deeper side of your character.

Control

The desire to control others often has its roots in problems about being controlled or being in situations beyond your personal control. Sometimes the desire to control derives from the unpleasant experience of being used and abused by someone else, perhaps in the past. This can cause you, from a psychological and emotional point of view, to want to ensure that this never happens again. In some cases, this is appropriate. For instance, if you had worked for a company that rode roughshod over employment law and practice, you would look to keep tight control over where you worked in the future. But control can also mean that you lose out on spontaneity and the joy of trusting those who care about you. If you know you seek to control most situations, try the following:

Once a week, ask your partner or a close friend to arrange a small surprise for you. It may be a meal out in a new restaurant or watching a video that you have never seen, but try to let them sort out all the details. Gradually increase the number of events you attend where others have had at least some element of control in the arrangements. It is possible that some mistakes will be made, but, in the bigger picture, this is a small price to pay for learning to trust others.

Blame

Using blame as a defence often begins if you have been punished by others for making mistakes. You may fear being caught out again, or live with the feeling that soon everyone will discover the real you – the person who fails or cannot make the grade. This is sometimes found in families where children blame parents for bringing them up to think or behave in a certain way, or in work places where the boss or another team member is made a scapegoat for a problem. Taking responsibility for personal concerns can be rewarding because it is often much easier to sort out difficulties if you act on the part of the problem you can solve, rather than waiting for everyone else to take responsibility for theirs. The well known saying, 'It is better to light a candle rather than to curse the darkness' is applicable to the blame culture. When you find yourself tempted to blame others, make a list of the parts of the issue for which you can take responsibility. Think about what you can actually do to make a change and do it. These small changes will help you to stop blaming others and avoid the defensive behaviour that often follows.

Withdrawal

Withdrawing as a defence is usually based on a fear of what may follow if you become involved – whether it is in an argument or debate, an event or relationship. Sometimes it follows a previous hurt – 'once bitten twice shy', as the saying goes. You withdraw quite simply to avoid the emotional complexity that may follow. You may feel safe in this situation, but you could also feel isolated and lonely. If you find you withdraw from potentially difficult situations, try asking yourself what you could contribute. It might be a hug, a kind word or a sympathetic ear. Build up this kind of involvement and you will slowly find it easier to relate to others. A bonus outcome will be that they are more likely to want to be involved with you, and this can make you feel much happier in the long run.

IN CONCLUSION

To be human is to have feelings and emotions. In order to have emotional self-esteem we need to achieve a balance in our emotional life. This chapter has dealt with common emotional problems that can cause an imbalance in feeling and behaviour and offered suggestions for dealing with this. Many people also use defences in order to maintain a healthy emotional self-esteem. Some defences are useful, whilst others inhibit intimate and loving relationships as well as affecting work performance and other areas of life. Learning about defences and how to overcome difficulties can help to achieve a balanced emotional life.

Chapter 5

MENTAL HEALTH AND SELF-ESTEEM

Positive mental health promotes a positive sense of self-esteem. If you feel good about yourself and are able to cope with the stress that everyday life can induce, you will be able to enjoy your relationships, work and leisure time. But many people increasingly find that stress and tiredness cause them to have mental health problems. The incidence of depression is on the increase, especially among women and young men (the Samaritans have found that actual and attempted suicide has almost tripled among young men since the mid 1980s).

This chapter will help you to identify common triggers for mental health problems and enable you to take action to boost your self-esteem by improving your mental attitude.

YOUR MENTAL HEALTH QUESTIONNAIRE

Now that you have filled in your mental health question-naire you are likely to have discovered areas that need some action and other areas that you feel confident about. Here are some of the areas that can cause stress and mental health concerns. All of them relate to the questionnaire so you might like to have a copy of your answers close at hand. Note how you answered the sections relating to the points below.

Changes in mood

Mood changes are normal and natural. Everybody has different moods and they can sometimes change for no apparent reason. However, if you experience frequent changes of mood – perhaps feeling up one moment and down the next – or feel stuck in one particular mood such as pessimism or frustration – you may find it much harder to tackle work tasks or feel close to your family. Of course, many mood changes are triggered by a particular event – a job loss, a bad trip to work, an argument with your partner, an invitation to a party, praise from your manager or just losing your car keys! If your questionnaire demonstrates that you change mood a great deal, or feel low much of the time, you may be under stress or feeling anxious. This will contribute to a loss of self-esteem.

Dealing with changes in mood

- *Look for the trigger to your mood fluctuations.* Do you experience a sinking feeling as you walk through the door of your place of work? Are you struggling to communicate successfully with your partner or family? Identifying the trigger to mood alterations is important because you may otherwise feel at the mercy of the changes, unable to control them. Discovering the cause can be the first step towards taking control of something you would like to alter, thereby improving your mood.

- *Notice if there is a pattern to your moods*. Are you better or worse at certain times of the day or week? Some people who suffer from depression and lethargy during the winter have benefited from 'light therapy' during this period. Lyn noticed that her moods changed considerably at the weekend. She often felt much more miserable and scratchy with her daughter. When she realised this was the case, she identified the visits from her ex-husband as the main cause of her feelings. He often phoned or called round when she was least expecting him, on a Saturday or Sunday, which she found hard to cope with. Once she had set up a pre-arranged system of visits from him to their little girl she felt much less unhappy and was able to enjoy her weekends.

- *Identify people who worsen or improve your mood change*. It may not always be possible to break with those who worsen your moods, but understanding the effect they have can be a way of resolving to alter patterns of behaviour. For example, Jill's neighbour often called in for coffee in the morning. Jill thought her neighbour was lonely and felt she owed it to her to be welcoming and friendly, but the neighbour, Margaret, was the kind of person who moaned constantly. Whatever the weather, Margaret would be fed up. After several months of Margaret's moaning about her family, friends, shopping trips, hairdresser – in fact, anything and everything – Jill decided to make some changes. Margaret's moaning usually left her feeling frustrated, annoyed and unhappy. Jill took a job in a local charity shop that meant she was not available every time Margaret called and also asked Margaret to call at other times when Jill's friends were visiting. This helped Jill to manage and share the burden of the situation and improved her mood. Jill did not want to cut Margaret off completely, as she realised Margaret needed support, but did need to take steps to halt the negative effect that Margaret had on her.

Responses to particular events

Many mental health problems are caused by self-esteem lowering responses to particular events. Some people seem to come through seemingly devastating events with few problems while others find themselves sinking into depression or chronic anxiety. This may be due to their personality or the kind of support they receive at the time. It is not unusual for people to 'punish' themselves for feeling sad or upset after a traumatic happening. Sometimes people tell themselves 'I must stop feeling like this' or, 'I must never let my partner know how I am feeling'. This approach can often make the feelings much worse, leading to (in some situations) serious mental health concerns. Learning how to respond to difficult situations is an important life skill, and can really improve mental self-esteem.

- *Trace your usual response to difficult events.* Do you tend to take cover, perhaps by shutting yourself away? Do you tell everyone who will listen? Do you look for someone to blame? Now decide if these approaches help or hinder your view of the situation or your self-esteem. If you find that others report your behaviour as hard to understand, maybe you are employing a defensive response (see Chapter 4 for more information on emotional defences).

• *Share your feelings with people you trust.* Men often find this more difficult than women, turning away from the 'touchy feely' stuff that they see as girl talk. Men may fear that their masculinity is under threat if they admit to feeling worried or depressed. The typical male response is to crush these feelings and to try to stay in control. But this approach does not help. In fact it makes things much worse. The concern can eat away at self-esteem, becoming a vicious circle that prevents solutions from being found. If you can learn to release difficult feelings gradually, like a valve on a pressure cooker, you will find you feel less bogged down by problems. If you feel there is no one to share your problems with, a Relate counsellor can help you to talk through your concerns and seek solutions that are right for you.

Coping with traumatic events

It is well known that traumatic life events can cause a deterioration in mental health and self-esteem. Bereavement, divorce and redundancy can all strike a blow to a positive view of yourself. Divorced men and women are likely to suffer from depression more than any other group. Here is how to manage the aftermath of a difficult life event.

- You may feel as if a great cloud of problems has descended upon you. This can have the effect of freezing you in your ability to take action. Instead of trying to manage every issue at once, try breaking the problem down into smaller 'bite-sized pieces'. For example, if you lose your job, deal with the things your employer should do about the redundancy before desperately searching for another job. Make lists of steps you need to take and tick off what you achieve.
- Allow yourself to feel sad or confused. This is a tough time and you have every right to experience some down days. (See Chapter 4 for more information on discussing feelings.)
- Do not be ashamed to seek help from support or counselling groups (Relate, for example) in your local area. In the UK it is often perceived as a personal failure to discuss worries with others. But this is a mistake. Most helping agencies have a great deal of expertise and experience in specialist areas.

Mental attitude

Some people interpret the words 'positive mental attitude' as a way of saying 'pull yourself together and stop whingeing'. But this is not the case. It simply means approaching problems (or life in general) with a positive attitude so that you can be more focused on thinking through what bugs you and take appropriate action.

- *Use positive thinking messages on yourself.* Instead of pulling yourself down with negative messages about 'I can't do this' or, 'I am not as clever as my friend/

relative/colleague'. Remind yourself of what you can do well. Avoid saying 'that's not very important' or, 'anyone can do that'. Be proud of what you can and do achieve, even if it is not nuclear physics!

- *List all the things you are proud of about yourself and stick them next to your mirror.* Every time you look in the mirror, you will see the list of things you really rate about yourself and this will boost your confidence.
- *Look for win/win situations in work or relationships.* Many negative attitudes actually originate from the idea that you have to win/be the best/come out on top and so on. Try thinking about problem-solving as team-work. This is particularly important for men who often feel uncertain about seeking assistance and believe they must achieve success alone.

TACKLING ANXIETY AND WORRY

Many mental health problems have their roots in high anxiety. Worry about work, family, relationships and health can all eat away at self confidence and lead to chronic anxiety – that is, worrying about several different things at the same time, desperately juggling your responsibilities and desires in a way that can eventually have a negative impact on your mental health.

Some people describe this as a vicious circle: the more they worry, the more they feel unable to tackle problem areas. Eventually, worry makes them feel as if they are living in a mental limbo, with little room for manoeuvre. Here are some ways to manage worry and anxiety so that they do not dominate your life. (See Chapter 8 for more information about anxiety and sex.)

1 Make a list of all the things you may be currently concerned about, or have responsibility for. For example, here is Gita's list:

- Caring for my elderly mother-in-law
- Keeping going in my part-time job
- Cooking and cleaning for my family
- Helping our sons through their school exams
- Supporting my husband in the family business
- Managing my asthma
- Concern for my oldest daughter who married recently
- Concern for my family in India
- Managing the morning coffee roster for the community support group at the local community centre
- Watching my weight
- Concern for endangered species in the world

Gita's list ranges from home-based issues to wider concerns. Many of her tasks require daily attention. Gita often feels tired, but finds it hard to ask for support from others as she feels she must take sole responsibility for all her tasks.

2 The next step is to divide the list into three categories, using the columns opposite. For instance, Gita might take immediate action on compiling the roster for the community centre rather than worrying about when she will find the time to do this. Gita also felt the time had come to discuss the care of her mother-in-law with her husband. She knew he would not feel happy about

finding other forms of care, but Gita knew that she needed help. Gita also wanted to be more involved in nature conservation, but felt unsure how to pursue this.

Action needed	Possible action	Future action
Create roster for community centre – put aside Tuesday mornings once a month.	Care for mother-in-law – talk to husband one evening this week.	Concern for endangered species – join Friends of the Earth or World Wildlife Fund for Nature.

Now fill in the columns with your own tasks.

3 Carry out all the tasks possible in the 'Action needed' column. Make sure that you enter tasks that are practical and achievable – and be specific. For instance, 'look for new job' is not specific and you will probably simply put it off. Instead, write 'buy local paper on the day the employment section appears'. Do not worry if your tasks appear small. Look for goals that will gradually lead you away from paralysing worry to real change where it is needed.

4 Now look at the middle column, headed 'Possible action'. In this column list the issues you have been meaning to tackle for a long time, perhaps those you are secretly worried will cause difficulties to others. Think about possible action you could take to reach an effective conclusion. As in the first column, do not worry if your task seems insignificant at first – just put down what you think would help to move this problem along. For instance, Kerry felt worried about her daughter who seemed withdrawn and distant. Instead of worrying about this and taking no action, Kerry noted that she would talk to her daughter's form teacher about her change in behaviour. Once she had carried out her task, Kerry discovered that her daughter was having some problems in adjusting to life at secondary school and was eventually able to work with the school to help her to feel more secure and supported.

5 In the last column, 'Future action' consider those worries that are more global and need a different kind of action from simply talking to a relative or work mate. Some people worry about world poverty or global

warming, and this can become an added concern on top of other, more personal concerns. You can find relief from this kind of anxiety by joining a charity, setting up a regular donation through a bank or by joining a local branch of a group that supports your concern.

You may find that some of your concerns do not fit easily into any column. For instance, Gita's cooking and cleaning duties seemed endless and needed dealing with every day. If you find the same, break the task down into smaller parts. For instance, Gita could decide to undertake particular tasks on particular days or ask her family to take a more active role in the housework. Daily concerns that lurk in your mind can clog up your response to other, probably 'one-off' decisions, that you need to take. This can give you the feeling that your life is full of trivia that never gets sorted out. Sorting these out, and giving them a real clean-up in the process, can make all the difference. Here is a list of the kind of concerns that really can be resolved if dealt with systematically.

- Housework (including food shopping and cooking)
- Filing and sorting household papers
- Organising children going to, and returning from, school
- Anything to do with cars – from servicing to regular filling with petrol
- Gardening
- Money issues – including organising direct debits, household accounts and the paying of bills
- Household storage – including deciding where clothes, kitchen items and keys are kept!

All of these tasks can be broken down and managed effectively. Worrying about whether the car should be serviced, what you will eat for dinner, how the children will get to school in the morning as well as trying to find yourself a new job that is better paid will mentally exhaust you. Remove some of the daily grind and the bigger issues will get the time they require.

Once you have started on this process of categorising your concerns, looking for appropriate action and breaking large tasks down into smaller ones, keep revisiting your list. Move your worries around, always seeking to get them into the first column (Action needed) in order to find an appropriate action that will shift the worry from your mind (where it is probably running round in a circle) and into the 'sorted' pile rather than the 'pending' tray!

STRESS – WHAT IT IS AND HOW TO PREVENT IT

Everywhere we look, people are talking about feeling 'stressed out', 'under stress' or simply 'full of stress'. It has become such a common term that we probably scarcely stop to consider what stress actually is and why it happens. According to the Department of Health (2000) eighty million working days are lost each year through emotional difficulties, with up to a quarter of the UK workforce affected by stress.

Most stress comes from our modern lifestyle. We were not meant to live in an environment that requires so many decision-making events every day. Our forebears had very few personal decisions to make. Most were decided by the clan or tribe and followed set patterns or rituals, such as following animal migration as nomads or setting up camps. Nowadays almost everything we do requires a personal decision, from the clothes we choose to put on in the morning to whom we live with. Added to this is the speed at which we are expected to make these decisions. Again, our ancestors could take their time over decision-making – following the seasons or time of day is much slower than watching the weather forecast on TV! We are surrounded by technology – mobile phones, PCs, the internet, voice mail – all designed to get us to communicate constantly with each other and to make decisions at a speed never dreamt of before. These advances have revolutionised our lives, but at a cost. Our ancient 'fight or flight' mechanism is stimulated by events that it was never intended to service. We can now experience a rush of adrenaline through being carved up on the motorway instead of chasing (or being chased by!) a large animal. Adrenaline prompts the body to act. It allows us to run from danger, respond at speed, or fight for what we wish to protect. In other words, it is concerned with physical action rather than mental action. Trapped in our car, feeling the surge of adrenaline, we cannot take the action that Stone Age man might have done. So this trapped response is then felt by us as stress. If this goes on over a sustained period of time (perhaps through feeling overworked and worried about the family), we start to show symptoms of stress. Here are some common stress symptoms:

- A feeling of tiredness that is not relieved by a good night's sleep or resting. This is sometimes called TATT – Tired All The Time.

- Feeling depressed and as if life is wearing you out. Sometimes you may feel wound-up, rushing from one area of life to another but never achieving what you set out to do.
- Stomach pains and digestion problems. Gastric problems have many different causes, so it is important to check out your concerns with a GP. Stress can make irritable bowel syndrome or discomfort in the stomach and duodenum much worse.
- Headaches, stiffness in the neck and shoulders, as well as back pain, can all be caused by stress, especially if it is ongoing. A visit to a GP about these symptoms is always worthwhile, if only to learn that some lifestyle changes could improve the situation.
- Domestic difficulties. Stress sufferers sometimes feel withdrawn from family life or easily become involved in arguments that escalate into steaming rows. They may over-react to issues that they otherwise would have ignored. For example, Erin became very angry with her son over his lost school bus money. After the row had become very heated, and both had eventually calmed down, Erin admitted that her anger had been fuelled by her worry about the problems her firm faced and the possibility that she could lose her job if it went into liquidation.
- Workaholicism. People who work all the hours available, and then still bring work home may be displaying symptoms of stress. Far from being motivated by the joy of work, they are more likely to be suffering from a real fear that unless they work very hard they will not keep up with their work colleagues. Anxiety-driven work can cause feelings of

impotence and a low self-image as work gradually consumes all of life.

- Sexual problems. Difficulties in sexual relationships can often be due to stress in other areas of life. More men and women than ever before are reporting loss of interest in sex and other kinds of sexual problems, including difficulties in getting and keeping an erection or reaching an orgasm. (See Chapter 8 for more information.)

HOW TO TACKLE STRESS

It may seem an odd thing to say but we all actually need some elements of stress in our lives. Without the motivation to deliver a piece of work on time, get the kids to school or simply to want to get up in the morning, little would happen. Our systems of government would grind to a halt and we would all turn into couch potatoes! The natural push of adrenaline to perform in some way is a human attribute and we do need it. But if we want to reduce the stress in our lives, we need to adapt the 'fight or flight' response to a modern setting. Here's how to do it:

- *Take exercise.* Many of us live very sedentary lifestyles. This means that when we repeatedly receive shots of adrenaline that are pushing us to action, but do nothing about them, stress levels climb. Regular exercise is very useful in dissipating stress. Choose physical activity that you are comfortable with rather than forcing yourself to undertake exercise you make yourself do out of a sense of duty. Walking, swimming, playing tennis or badminton and other kinds of exercise, such as judo, tai-chi or yoga can all be beneficial. Avoid taking part in fiercely competitive squash or tennis ladders or sports that simply increase your stress level. Remember, you are not there to 'perform', simply to work off the stress you have accrued during the day. Simple physical tasks – such as gardening – can be extremely stress reducing, as can kneading dough or clearing out the attic. (See Chapter 3 for more information about exercise.)

- *Relax*. This does *not* mean dashing to the masseur, having your muscular knots undone, only to race back to your desk so that you can get on with work! *Or* drinking far too much on a Friday night in a bid to relax and switch off the events of the week before. True relaxation means letting go and chilling out. Make sure you mark time in your diary that is just for you and those you love. Do not be tempted to book meetings during that time because your 'family will understand'. They won't and you will not only feel exhausted but also have to deal with the animosity of your partner and children because you are never where you say you will be. At the end of their life, no one ever said 'I wish I had spent more time at the office or factory'! Take all your holiday allowance, spend weekends doing something that refreshes you. Slumping in front of the TV is not a good form of relaxation (except occasionally). Reading or listening to gentle music is a better option as this has a calming effect.
- *Undertake some 'life analysis'*. If your relationships are in a mess, or you feel worn out by caring for a baby or

elderly parent, your stress levels can rise. Look at the different areas of your life and try to see if any of these are stressful because you have been too tired or busy to sort out some support or to try different approaches. Even if you know you are always going to be the principal carer for your frail mother, for instance, it is important to ensure that you find the support you need. Check that you, or the person you care for, is receiving all the benefits you are both entitled to and explore the possibility of respite care. A short break can help you to cope with the demands of being a carer.

If you feel your relationship is collapsing, consider going to see a Relate counsellor. Investing time and money in a course of counselling can be very good value. Most people who come to Relate have an average of six sessions. Eighty per cent of people who attend say that Relate counselling meets their needs. Relate has also undertaken research to find out whether stress levels are reduced by their counselling. The research demonstrates that even those who are extremely stressed at the start of counselling have significantly lower stress levels at the close of counselling – in some cases, stress levels dropped by two-thirds.

Do not be afraid to ask others for some support and help. It is common for new parents to imagine they have to manage alone. Talk to your health visitor or GP and enlist the assistance of family and friends in babysitting or in sharing care. A short walk in the local park while a grandparent or trusted friend minds your child can help you to feel better and less wound-up. Ask your partner to accompany you and you will have extra time to indulge in an adult conversation. This is especially important if you have spent the whole day conversing in gurgles – fun, but not intellectually stimulating!

WHEN TO SEEK HELP FOR MENTAL HEALTH CONCERNS

Although it is of course possible to feel low or stressed for some time without developing a mental illness, there are times when sustained problems can lead to a mental health difficulty. If you recognise any of the following signs in yourself, partner, friend or family member, seek medical help as soon as possible:

- *Difficulty in sleeping.* Waking very early, and then feeling sluggish all day, is a common symptom of depression. Problems in getting to sleep, followed by waking through the night can indicate high anxiety levels.
- *General tiredness and lethargy.* Feeling that everything is too much trouble or stressful can indicate depression, as can taking less interest in caring for one's self. This includes changes in dressing or bathing routines. For example, Yvonne became very worried about her brother when he stopped dressing and simply wore his dressing gown all day without shaving. As a man who had previously been punctilious about his appearance, his change in habit indicated to Yvonne that something serious had altered in his life. In fact, he had lost his job and his self-esteem had plummeted.

- *Changes in eating and drinking habits.* Some people who are severely depressed eat or drink very little. Others 'comfort eat' – that is, they pick at (often) sugary foods in order to subdue the feelings of misery that they are feeling. This can become a vicious circle where they eat, feel guilty for eating too much, and suffer a deeper loss of self-esteem. Other examples include an increase in alcohol consumption and drug abuse. Feelings of self hatred or unhappiness often trigger excessive alcohol consumption because alcohol anaesthetises emotion and creates a temporary escape from the reality of depression. This is usually very short-lived, and once the binge is over the individual may find the 're-entry' to normal life much worse than prior to the drinking bout.

- *A lack of communication.* If your partner normally spends time talking to you about their feelings and thoughts, but begins to seem distant and unresponsive, they may be preoccupied with feelings of unhappiness. This is especially true if they have recently faced an emotionally challenging situation. For instance, sustained withdrawal following a bereavement or divorce, house move, childbirth or job change (sometimes an improvement in a career) can all lead to changes in self-esteem.

- *Suicidal feelings.* Although this may seem an extreme, there is little reason to believe that people who talk about suicide do not attempt it. Many who describe wanting to end their life, or who talk about how they would actually go about ending their life, really intend to try it out. If your partner or friend tells you they feel suicidal you should treat it as a serious intent. Seek help from the experts in this area, the Samaritans.

- *Frequent marked changes in emotions.* Some people suffering from mental illness move from one state of emotion to another, often swinging wildly from euphoria to the depths of despair. This can make the sufferer feel as if they are caught up in an emotional storm that leaves them feeling exhausted and hard to communicate with.

Many of the symptoms above can be experienced in everyday life. Most of us know what it is like to have 'down' days, but if any of the above lasts more than a few weeks, or seems to happen regularly over months, seek help from a GP or other medical professional because speedy help for mental health concerns can often prevent a more serious problem from developing.

IN CONCLUSION

This chapter has considered the issues concerning mental health self-esteem. It has focused particularly on changes in mood and our responses to events around us, including trauma. It has also looked at maintaining a positive mental attitude and dealing with anxiety and stress.

Section II
LOVING ANOTHER

Chapter 6

CREATING COUPLE-ESTEEM

The first section of this book dealt with individual self-esteem from a physical, emotional and mental standpoint. In this section, we will explore the notion of 'couple-esteem'. Loving yourself is important because without a positive self regard you may find it hard to love another. Couple-esteem is about integrating your sense of self-esteem in a partnership in order to create a relationship that nurtures you and that is fulfilling and emotionally secure. Not all relationships allow this to happen – some partnerships are based not on equal mutual regard, but on fear of loneliness or anxiety about the future. This section will help you to understand how to love another person, what kind of relationship you have, and how to boost your couple-esteem.

LEARNING TO LOVE

How did you learn to love? This might seem a strange question, but everybody 'learns' how to love. Usually we take our first lessons from our parents. If our parents are responsive and caring, we learn that it is all right to trust another person. If they seem distant or uncaring, we may learn that love is not always reliable. Most of all, we need parents and carers who are able to give appropriate love at the right time. This means being protective and anticipating our physical and emotional needs when we are young, and being able to let go when we are older, giving us room to make our own successes (and mistakes). From these experiences we observe how to speak to a loved one, offer care and support and how to laugh with people we care for.

Here are some common parenting styles. These styles are rather like the story of Goldilocks and the three bears – some families are emotionally charged (hot), some are distant and emotionally flat (cold) and some are able to adjust to the needs of the child (just right). As you read, try to decide if your upbringing fits these descriptions and if your emotional porridge was hot, cold or just right! Answer the questions before you read the answer that is most appropriate to you:

FAMILY STYLE
ONE

1 As a child, did your family sometimes seem overbearing? Y/N
2 Did you occasionally feel overwhelmed by the hurly-burly of family life? Y/N
3 Do you recall a lot of affection and warmth? Y/N
4 How did you feel about this affection – for instance, did it sometimes seem constricting? Y/N
5 Did the affection help you to feel close to your parents/ carers? Y/N

6   Did your parents tell you they expected you to do well at school?   Y/N
7   Were you an only child?   Y/N
8   Did you sometimes have to step carefully to avoid parental emotional storms?   Y/N
9   Do you feel, looking back to your time as a child, that your parents expected you to please them?   Y/N
10 Did you long to rebel, but felt afraid to?   Y/N
11 Do you feel that, when the time came to leave home, you could only get away after an argument (or similar showdown)?   Y/N
12 Did you often feel the centre of attention?   Y/N
13 Did either parent tell you that they had only stayed in the marriage/partnership 'for your sake' or 'for the children'?   Y/N
14 Were you expected to hold the same kind of views as your family and their friends?   Y/N
15 Did you know you were loved, but sometimes felt under pressure in the family?   Y/N
16 Were cuddling and physical affection important in the family?   Y/N
17 Did you sometimes wish your parents/carers were less 'interfering'?   Y/N
18 Did your family take quite a long time to adjust to you having boy- or girlfriends?   Y/N
19 Do you still keep some secrets from your parents/carers?   Y/N
20 Do you still find it hard to express views that are different from the views your parents/carers brought you up to hold?   Y?N

Mostly 'yes'

If you answered mostly 'yes' to the questions above, your family may have been rather like a hot-house, with you (and possibly your siblings) as the precious plants. Your family loved you, but also expected certain returns from you – a good performance at school or university, for instance. Part of you may have enjoyed this special attention, but another part of you may have longed to be less restricted and more able to express a different side of your character. You may also have been expected to demonstrate a fierce family loyalty, agreeing with any shared views – perhaps political or religious – the family discussed or lived by. You may have also felt that the relationship between your parents was volatile. That is, it was prone to emotional outbursts, or may have even seemed unhappy, especially if the focus on you was because the relationship between your carers/parents was so difficult that you became the centre of their (or just one parent's) life.

If you were brought up in a single parent household you may have felt pressure to meet your parent's emotional needs in order to fulfil their dreams rather than your own needs. From these experiences you may regard emotional intimacy with some ambiguity – you want a close and loving relationship, but are also wary of the control you fear could be exercised over you if you form such a relationship. You may choose partners who are cool or undemanding, or form a relationship that emulates that of your parents, where your partner calls the shots and you follow. This is because the pull of the familiar is extremely powerful, whether you choose to avoid it at all costs or actively seek a similar situation. As a hot-house product, you are likely to want to succeed and this can help you in your chosen couple relationship as you will actively seek solutions to problems.

———— FAMILY STYLE ————
TWO

1   As a child, did your family sometimes seem uninterested in you and your achievements?   Y/N

2   Did you often have to fall back on your own resources rather than ask your parents/carers for assistance?   Y/N

3   Was physical affection (hugs, cuddles and general emotional warmth) in short supply?   Y/N

4   Did you want more affection?   Y/N

5   Was yours a large family with several brothers and sisters, or other relatives living with you?   Y/N

6   Did you sometimes push against acceptable behaviour boundaries in order to get a response?   Y/N

7   Did you often feel closer to friends than your own family?   Y/N

8   Do you feel, looking back, that you would have liked more 'hands on' advice from your parents as you were growing up?   Y/N

9   Did you tend to have role models outside the family – teachers, youth group leaders, etc?   Y/N

10 Do you regard yourself as a 'self starter' – usually highly motivated?   Y/N

11 Were your parents cool towards one another – that is, seemingly physically unaffectionate towards one another?   Y/N

12 Do you find it hard to depend on others?   Y/N

13 Do you tend to believe that there is only one person you can really trust, and that is you?   Y/N

14 Are you close to your siblings?   Y/N

15 At social events do you sometimes feel out on a limb, or the odd one out?   Y/N

16 Are you a determined person who tries hard to see things through, even if others do not agree with or support you?   Y/N

17 Are you are a tidy person, with a place for everything? Y/N
18 Do you believe it is important for children to be given clear messages about their behaviour at all times?   Y/N
19 As an adult, are you still not sure if you know (knew) your parents very well?   Y/N

Mostly 'yes'

Unlike the hot-house environment of Family Syle One, you were raised as a hardy plant, expected to survive whatever the weather. Your parents did care for you, but were probably not very affectionate because they found it embarrassing or were not themselves brought up to show love in a demonstrative manner. As a young person, you may have actively looked for more affection, or simply accepted that your family's emotional style was 'normal'. If your parents seemed uninterested in your life – perhaps by not attending school events or praising your achievements – you may have tried to gain their attention by other means. Some people who feel their parents/carers show little interest in them tend to rebel, demanding attention by getting expelled from school, dressing flamboyantly or taking risks such as drinking and drug taking when teenagers. Others try extremely hard to demonstrate their abilities by working very hard at their exams.

As an adult you may find it hard to trust others, or believe that friends have a special interest in you. Your self-esteem can be quite low at times, especially if you have to rely on others for assistance. This could be because you have spent a lot of time relying on yourself and feel it is an admission of failure to ask others for help. You tend to look for partnerships where you can be in control or where the relationship is at arm's length – perhaps in an internet 'on-line' relationship. In order to replace some of the warmth you missed in childhood, you may seek a partner who is overtly affectionate or extrovert. You may feel close to your siblings because they were supportive in situations where your parents were not, or distant from them because you have developed a protective skin against the uncomfortable feelings that intimacy can bring to the surface.

───────── FAMILY STYLE ─────────
THREE

1   Do you feel that both parents offered you warmth and encouragement most of the time?   Y/N
2   In general, while you were growing up, was there little overt competition between you and your siblings for your parents' attention?   Y/N
3   Were you normally encouraged to voice your opinions? Y/N
4   Did you know where the family boundaries lay in terms of acceptable behaviour and conduct?   Y/N
5   Were these boundaries arrived at in discussion with you rather than simply imposed?   Y/N
6   Did you feel that you received physical affection appropriate to your age and circumstances?   Y/N
7   Were your parents physically demonstrative to one another?   Y/N
8   Were there some arguments in the family where the anger was not seen as destructive in emotional terms? Y/N

9 Are you usually confident with groups of strangers? Y/N

10 Do you find it easy to trust people? Y/N

11 Have you had reasonably good relationships with your siblings? Y/N

12 Were you shown love and affection even when you made mistakes? Y/N

13 Were you and your family able to say sorry to each other after disagreements or problems? Y/N

14 As an adult, do you have reasonably good relationships with your siblings? Y/N

15 Are you able to show affection to others fairly easily, when appropriate? Y/N

16 Can you offer an opinion to others without feeling anxious about how it will be received? Y/N

17 Are you willing to listen to the ideas of others? Y/N

18 As a teenager, did you feel able to accept or reject your parents' views without feeling either crushed or ignored? Y/N

19 Can you express anger without fearing that it will spiral out of control? Y/N

Mostly 'yes'

Family Style Three is one where adults and children feel as if they are part of a team – pulling together to create a home that is supportive and affectionate. This is not to suggest that this type of family does not encounter problems. They often have just as many difficulties as other families, but tackle them in a way that allows each family member to feel that their views have been taken into account. Perhaps the key to Family Style Three is a willingness to imagine what it is like to be another member of the family. For instance, they are able to empathise with a screaming toddler who does not want to go to bed, rather than simply ignoring the frustration the child feels. However, this does not mean that they will abandon their personal rules – that the toddler should go to bed, for instance – but that they will enforce them in an affectionate and understanding manner. Treating others in the way you would like to be treated is important because it demonstrates the care that most families (in any of the three styles) would like to feel they have for each other.

If you were brought up in a family like this, you will have a real ability to understand others and will choose partners by assessing their behaviour, rather than simply being motivated by a romantic dream or lust! Your self-esteem will be good because you will have experienced a family life that allowed you to feel good about yourself, and dealt successfully with any experiences that may have lowered your self-esteem. In essence, this kind of family provides their children with an emotional 'tool box'. The tools can be used to repair hurt or to make sense of new relationships as the child grows and develops.

Now that you have read the questions, and decided which style you most identify with, you can begin to understand how family upbringing can influence your choice of partner. The next section will ask you to think about your present and past relationships so that you can begin to assess how you maintain your 'couple-esteem', and go on to improve this if you feel it is not as good as you would like it to be.

142   *Loving Yourself Loving Another*

LEARNING FROM PAST RELATIONSHIPS

Do you feel that your past relationships conform to a pattern? Many people tell Relate counsellors that they feel they repeat patterns in partnerships, sometimes making the same mistakes. For instance, Mark felt that he went into new relationships too quickly, diving headlong into commitment before he fully realised the consequences or really knew the girl properly. Each time he did this he told himself it would never happen again, only to repeat the process! For some this repeating pattern seems to stop a new relationship in its tracks as one or both partners realise what is happening. For others, a repeating pattern feels like a maze that is impossible to escape from. Here are some common repeating patterns. Try to decide if you identify with any of these:

The Pursuer

The Pursuer tends to chase the person he or she would like to form a relationship with regardless of the responses he or she receives. In fact, the more the object of their desire seems to demur, the harder they chase. Pursuers tend to put a great deal of effort into the 'courtship' phase of the relationship, sometimes ignoring the possible future relationship. Once the relationship is established and the pursuit scaled down, the pursuer often loses interest. The person who has been pursued can experience confusion and disappointment, feeling that they have been duped as the emotional intensity cools down.

The Clinger

The Clinger often hangs onto a relationship regardless of what is happening in it. Clingers may behave as if they are emotionally blind, sometimes excusing their partners of behaviour that most people would feel was inexcusable. Clingers are often afraid of launching out into the world alone and fear new partnerships. They may suffer from low self-esteem, believing that they will not find another relationship of any value. They will stay in failing partnerships despite warnings from others that the partnership is about to crash. Sometimes, even when the relationship has actually ended, Clingers will make repeated attempts to revive it, even if their ex-partner rebuffs them.

The Cool Customer

The Cool Customer never wears his/her heart on his/her sleeve. She/he tends to leave his partner guessing about his feelings and to avoid declaring them as much as possible. This sometimes lends Cool Customers a mysterious air of allure that can seem attractive, or opens the door to a partnership between a Pursuer and a Cool Customer that turns into an almost constant game of 'cat and mouse'. Sometimes Cool Customers have been hurt in previous relationships and have learnt to shield their feelings to avoid being trampled on again.

The Open Heart

The Open Heart is precisely what it describes. Open Hearts are likely to have their feelings on show all the time. Although initially this may seem quite beguiling, it can often wear partners down as they try to keep up with the shifts of emotion that can occur from one day to the next. Strangely, Open Hearts may link up with Cool Customers, becoming more and more emotional as the Cool Customer becomes less and less so in response. They may demand demonstrations of affection or feeling and become very frustrated when these are not forthcoming.

The Broken Record

The Broken Record relationship occurs when a traumatic event rocks a couple (perhaps a serious illness or an affair) and is not acknowledged. The couple then seem to become stuck in a groove of behaviour – perhaps recrimination or anger – for months, sometimes years. This behaviour usually results from a fear of tackling the problem head-on, and actually stops the pair from understanding the wider implications of the event. The 'groove' acts as a defence, allowing the couple to stay together (however unhappily) without examining their feelings about what has happened.

The Appeaser

Similar in character to the Clinger, the Appeaser often acts as a go-between. Appeasers may try to act as an intermediate between their partner and the world, preventing difficult situations from touching their partner, or even screening out issues they perceive as a threat to the relationship. For instance, many Appeasers carry messages to a partner's family, particularly if there has been a split or feud between the partner and his or her relatives. Appeasers sometimes seek to cool down angry situations by asking others – children, for instance – to amend their behaviour around a partner so as not to provoke an unwanted emotional situation. Appeasing and interpreting for a partner can carry a reward in the form of power and control. Appeasers can get others to behave or respond in a particular way to their partners, and friends and relations may stop bothering to comm- unicate directly with their partners, using the Appeasers instead.

The Provoker

Relationships involving a strong Provoker partner can look prickly and difficult to the outsider, but may actually be sound. Provokers can cause a relationship to be full of ups and downs because no issue is ever left untouched. Both partners may feel as if they are constantly wrestling with some kind of decision, idea or expectation. For instance, Clive wanted to decide where the family were to go on holiday the following year. He asked his partner repeatedly about the holiday, urging her to apply for leave from work, bringing home holiday brochures every day and raising the subject at each meal time for a month. Eventually the family made a decision, although the holiday was months away! Provokers can also push partners to talk about feelings or future hopes. Sometimes this can be helpful, but more often it can be intrusive and annoying. Provokers teamed with

Appeasers can be a recipe for disaster as the Provoker may simply push the Appeaser further and further until the Appeaser cannot cope with trying to stand between the Provoker and his or her family or friends. Provokers may also demand a great deal of attention, making their partners feel cut off from their own relatives. Provokers often feel insecure about their place in life, believing that others do not value them, so they have to make their position clear by the demands they make.

The Dependent

The Dependent relationship is based on one partner depending strongly on the other. The traditional couple of the twentieth century consisted of a dependent woman looking to a strong man to get her through life in a variety of ways, including financially, practically and emotionally. Nowadays, this stereotypical model has been rightly challenged, but many couples still consist of one person who depends upon the other, often as a protector. Both partners can gain from this arrangement – the Dependent gets to be looked after while the Protector feels important and needed. It can also act as emotional glue – both partners may be afraid to leave the relationship as the Dependent will feel 'I can't go because I do not know how I will manage alone' and the protector partner will feel 'I must stay because he/she needs me to look after him/her'.

These descriptions of different styles of relationships may not absolutely fit yours. In fact, you may find that parts of different categories apply to you. This is quite normal. You may identify your own relationship style and discover that your partner fits one of the individual roles while you fit another. All of these combinations have strengths and weaknesses, but exploring and understanding how they interact can help you to bolster your particular partnership.

YOUR EXPECTATIONS OF YOUR RELATIONSHIP

Every couple relationship is constructed from the basic building bricks of expectations and hopes for the future. Some of these may be openly discussed – such as the desire to have (or not have) children. Others may be unspoken, even unconscious – such as a desire for a partner to be faithful or to meet particular sexual desires. As the relationship develops, these expectations can affect your personal 'couple-esteem'. If your expectations are met, you are likely to regard your relationship in a positive light. If not, you may decide the partnership is failing.

Case Study

Harry and Naomi met through mutual friends. They both enjoyed sport and their first date was spent cheering on their local football team. Both played badminton and attended a local gym. Harry had been very turned on by Naomi's lithe body, honed by regular physical exercise. He expected that this would always be the case and relished the idea that they would go on exercising and enjoying sport together. Naomi privately felt differently. She certainly enjoyed sport, but also wanted to have a baby. When Harry proposed they married quickly and Naomi became pregnant almost immediately. Harry felt ambiguous about this – he had wanted to wait a while before becoming a father. As the pregnancy proceeded, Naomi withdrew from the frequent gym trips, leaving Harry to go alone. She also stopped accompanying him to football matches as she felt uncomfortable on the seats in the stand. Harry was not happy about this, but was more unhappy about the changes to Naomi's body. He did not tell Naomi that he found her growing stomach unattractive, and that he missed her sporty look of their pre-marriage days. They began to argue, often over small daily annoyances, but never over Harry's true concern, the coming child or the change in Naomi. Naomi felt puzzled as she believed that Harry shared her desire to have a baby, while Harry felt he could not raise the issue about Naomi's altered attitude to the very thing that brought them together – sport. Once the baby – a girl – was born, Harry hoped that Naomi would begin to make time to get back to sport. But Naomi showed no sign of doing this. Harry began to wonder if the marriage could carry on, while Naomi felt that Harry was inconsiderate and uncaring towards her.

Naomi and Harry had a set of expectations that were hardly discussed before they married. Here are some of them:

Harry's expectations	Naomi's expectations
Naomi would maintain the sporty, sexy body that turned him on.	Harry would continue to find her attractive as her body changed.
They would discuss becoming parents at some time in the future.	Harry wanted children as quickly as she did.
They would continue to enjoy attending, and taking part in, sport together.	They would experience a change in priorities once they were married, and engage in fewer sporting activities.
Parenthood would not change their key shared pleasures.	Becoming parents would bring about change that they would need to assimilate.

Harry and Naomi also had different ideas about how their couple relationship should look. Harry saw them as an independent, lively, sporty, sexually active couple who might be parents at some point in the future. Naomi enjoyed the sporty image they shared, but also wanted them to become parents quickly and was less concerned about being independent. She also placed less emphasis on the sexual aspects of their relationship, seeing this as just one part of the way they related to each other rather than a mainstay of their shared image of themselves.

The image that you hold in your head about what your relationship should look like or how it was constructed in the first place can affect your shared couple esteem. Try the following task to see what the building blocks of your relationship might be, and how this leads to a shared image for the two of you.

Using the table below, tick those elements that formed some of your expectations of your relationship. You may also like to add some of your own at the end of the list that may not have been covered:

Expectations and 'building blocks'	Tick here if you agree this was one of your expectations and 'building blocks'
Faithfulness	
Financial security	
To become parents	
To live together	
To get married	
Both partners to carry on working or to follow a chosen career	
To support partner if they wish to study instead of work	
To carry on with hobbies/interests/other pursuits, etc	
To maintain a regular and satisfying sexual relationship	
To have harmonious relationships with each other's parents and extended families	
To maintain some degree of social independence – e.g. to continue to have evenings out with friends	

Expectations and 'building blocks'	Tick here if you agree this was one of your expectations and 'building blocks'
To give up certain activities or friendships after moving in together or getting married	
To share domestic tasks equally	
To take shared holidays rather than independent breaks	
To spend Christmas in a particular style – e.g. visiting one set of parents or opening gifts at a set time	
To buy a home together	

Once you have ticked those items that match your expectations for the relationship, try asking your partner to do the same thing. You might discover some surprises! Most couples will have a number of shared building blocks, with others that are extremely personal. It is probably impossible to try to agree on everything, but hidden expectations that are unfulfilled (as with Harry and Naomi) can undermine the success of your relationship.

ENSURING YOU HAVE SHARED EXPECTATIONS

If you are new to your relationship, understanding what your expectations mean to you as a couple is crucial. Even if your relationship is well established, you may still have expectations of your partner. These may have changed over the years, or be the same as those that you held when you first got together. Here is how to understand what your shared expectations are and how to fulfil them.

List your expectations

Use the list above to help you, and add your individual expectations. For instance, Toni knew that her mother needed nursing support and wanted her fiancé Dan to agree to have her mother living with them. Once you have created your list, decide if any of the topics have not been openly discussed or shared in some way.

Make time to talk

Find some time to share what you have discovered. Be aware that this may come as a surprise to your partner, so explain what has prompted you to think about this issue. You could prepare the way for this by asking your partner to fill in the list of expectations above. It is possible that your partner may not place the same emphasis on certain hopes about the relationship as you do. The aim of talking to each other about hopes and dreams about the future of the relationship is not to conduct a witch hunt, demanding that your partner gives you what you think is missing, but to decide together if your expectations are still relevant and/or need re-evaluating.

Renegotiate

All relationships change. This means that your expectations, although valid at the start of the partnership, could need revamping later. If you discover that some of your expectations and building blocks have been knocked around a bit, or never really got off the ground, renegotiating some shared ideals can really help you to feel closer to one another, as well as boosting your couple-esteem. For example, Ivan and Bobby had always felt that a love of travel was important to their relationship. As the years passed, and a shared business took up more and more of their time, this aspiration gradually disappeared. After Ivan re-evaluated what had been an important part of their joint life, they decided to try and book some time for a holiday. You may also want to add in any issues that have come to the surface since you became a couple. For example, you may wish to talk about how money is divided or how you feel about your sex life together.

Take action

It is easy to feel that just talking about the expectations you once had, and would like to revive, is enough to change your relationship for the better. You might easily assume that now that your partner knows that you would like to revisit some aspect of your partnership, everything will be all right. Unfortunately, merely talking is often not enough to make a real difference. Yes, you will understand more about what you want or need, and your partner's viewpoint, but nothing will happen if you do not decide on affirmative action. For example, you may decide that one of the basic building blocks of your relationship was a mutual love of classical music. Now you need to book a concert, buy a new CD or make sure you listen to classics on the radio. Maybe you could explore joining a local choir or music appreciation society. This may mean making special arrangements, such as finding a babysitter, so talk about who will do this rather than assuming that just one partner will do all the work. Taking action in this way can put you back in touch with what gave you couple-esteem in the past, as well as allowing you to experiment with new interests. After all, if you discover you now hate Beethoven, you no longer need to feel resentful that your partner never takes you to concerts any more!

IN CONCLUSION

This chapter has introduced the notion of couple-esteem. Every couple has a different style of interacting. Understanding how you interact with your partner can help you to understand the building blocks of your relationship and their relevance to you today – whether the relationship has lasted years or only just begun.

Chapter 7

MAKING COUPLE-ESTEEM WORK FOR YOU

What makes you feel fulfilled in your relationship? You might find you can answer this easily, citing lots of happy memories or instances. Or you may find it much harder to quantify. Maybe it has been some while since you felt you had real couple-esteem. Whatever your feelings, this chapter is aimed at helping you to make couple-esteem work in your favour so that you have a partnership that feels as if you are both pulling in the same direction rather than pulling apart.

THE STATE OF THE NATION

Every year the President of the USA gives a 'state of the nation' address. He (but not she – yet!) sums up how things are going in America from a fiscal and policy point of view. This is intended to inform the country about the direction in which the citizens are headed as well as how things have been during the previous year. In the same way, you can examine the state of your relationship, looking at how things have been, how they are, and where you are headed in the future.

Look at the questions below and answer 'yes' or 'no' to the questions, calculating your score as you proceed. The assessment after the quiz will help you to make sense of what is happening in your relationship, together with suggestions for improvements you might make to boost your couple-esteem.

---

1   We can talk to each other easily about a variety of topics.
    Y = 1, N = 0
2   We regularly put time aside to be together alone.   Y = 1,
    N = 0
3   There are taboo subjects we find hard to discuss that can
    cause problems if they are aired.   Y = 0, N = 1
4   We both know about our financial arrangements and
    discuss the best way to spend or save our cash.   Y = 1,
    N = 0
5   We made a joint, planned decision to have, or not have,
    children.   Y = 1, N = 0
6   We are able to be affectionate towards each other on a reg-
    ular basis.   Y = 1, N = 0
7   When we talk about difficult subjects we frequently argue
    or have prolonged periods without talking afterwards.
    Y = 0, N = 1
8   On the whole, we are sexually compatible.   Y = 1, N = 0
9   We do not talk about sex at all, or if we do it usually ends
    in a row.   Y = 0, N = 1
10 We still share interests that brought us together.   Y = 1,
    N = 0
11 We talk about hopes for the future.   Y = 1, N = 0
12 There have been instances of aggression or violence in our
    relationship.   Y = 0, N = 1

13 We have a shared group of friends whom we feel support us if we have any difficulties.   Y = 1, N = 0

14 Both of us have reasonably good relationships with each other's families.   Y = 1, N = 0

15 There is room for appropriate personal independence in our relationship.   Y = 1, N = 0

16 We share domestic tasks in a way that suits both of us. Y = 1, N = 0

17 Although we both work, just one of us undertakes the majority of the domestic tasks in the house.   Y = 0, N = 1

18 We have a lively shared sense of humour.   Y = 1, N = 0

19 We respect each other's viewpoint most of the time. Y = 1, N = 0

20 *Answer this question if you have children* When the children leave home, we will still have a meaningful relationship.   Y = 1, N = 0

Score totals 5 to 9

Your relationship needs some urgent attention. You may feel frustrated or out of touch with what drew you together in the first place. It is possible that you have been through a difficult period – perhaps a bereavement or a job problem – that has cast a negative influence over your relationship. Look back at the 'building blocks' section in Chapter 6 and assess how you may need to renegotiate those areas that seem shaky. Of particular concern are topics concerned with communication. Most problems stem from an inability to talk and listen to one another because sorting out how you will resolve problems always needs effective communication. Consider seeing a Relate counsellor, especially if you have answered 'yes' to question 12.

Score totals 10 to 14

You have a relationship that has moderate couple-esteem, but is very likely to have particular 'no go' areas. Look back at the questions and note the topics to which you have answered in the negative. You will probably find that there are issues you know you avoid or have never really tackled (such as sex, money, or parenting) that need some form of resolution. Raising your couple-esteem means sorting out long-running concerns rather than allowing them to eat away at the foundations of your partnership.

Score totals 15 to 20

You already have a high-esteem relationship, and obviously invest a lot of time and effort in it. Now is the perfect time to think through what you want for the future. Look at the questions that you have answered in the negative and try to understand what they are saying about your partnership. For instance, you may have answered 'no' to question 16. If so, this is an area that needs some attention. Sometimes a couple who communicate well run into difficulties over a particular issue because of a change in their partnership. For instance, Kay and Mel found they got out of the habit of cleaning their shared flat in an equal way after Mel decided to work part time. Kay decided that she could do the majority of the housework as she was at home more than her. This caused some rows before they realised what had happened. Once Kay saw she had made a false set of assumptions, and Mel realised what had happened, they divided the household tasks up in a way that suited them both after their change in work styles.

Assessing your relationship in this way may seem unromantic or 'too clinical' – as if you are both rats in a laboratory! But if you gradually become more attuned to what is happening in your partnership, you will find you can take immediate steps to resolve a problem or be more positive. After all, small corrections while steering a car are often unnoticed by the driver because they are almost automatic. Drivers are constantly checking their position on the road and assessing their speed. If drivers only ever took corrective action when the car began to veer into the kerb, we would wonder if they should be driving a car at all. It is the same with a couple relationship. Small adjustments undertaken on a daily basis may be barely noticed, whereas trying to correct a major problem that has been neglected for months or years can be extremely difficult.

THE TEN INDICATORS OF HIGH COUPLE-ESTEEM

The famous novelist, Count Leo Tolstoy, began his book *Anna Karenina* with the statement, 'All happy families are alike but an unhappy family is unhappy after its own fashion'. This is a well known quote that carries a great deal of truth, especially as recent research into what makes a contented (or discontented) couple seems to indicate that successful relationships do have similar characteristics. Here are 10 of the most common:

1 *A sense of mutual respect.* Each partner offers the other a high degree of respect, valuing their opinion and seeking their help over problems and difficulties.

2 *A team approach.* The couple see themselves as 'we', rather than two separate entities who happen to live together. They have a strong shared vision of what they both stand for, and agree on issues that affect them most strongly – such as parenting and financial arrangements.

3 *An ability to adapt to change.* Rather than sticking to rigid ideas about what should happen in a given situation, the successful couple create strategies to deal with different circumstances throughout a variety of life stages. They tend to treat each situation as an interesting challenge, rather than trying to force a situation to conform to pre-set and static rules.

4 *A mutual affection.* This may seem rather obvious – surely all couples are affectionate to one another? The truth is that some people never demonstrate affection. This has nothing to do with a sexual relationship (although regular hugs and kisses do help to make sex more enjoyable). A cuddle, a word of praise and a sense of warmth towards a partner can help to maintain an intimate bond that allows the couple to feel close and loving.

5 *A good memory for the past.* Intriguingly, the ability to recall events that were important to the couple seems to indicate a good couple bond. This does seem to make sense if you think about this shared memory as part of the process of creating a 'couple entity' (see point two above) rather than two separate people to whom the past is a private memory.

Talking about and recalling a first kiss, a special piece of music, the first place ever lived in together or a wonderful wedding day helps a couple to see themselves as special and unique.

6 *A shared set of values.* Couples who have a similar outlook on life tend to disagree less than those who are attracted to each other but have widely differing opinions or beliefs. This is not to say that opposites cannot make a happy relationship, but most individuals stand a better chance if they team up with someone who broadly shares their approach to life. For instance, a vegetarian with strong feelings about ecology and conservation *could* have a relationship with a dyed-in-the-wool carnivore who preferred concrete to green meadows, but the partnership would probably end in tears!

7 *A willingness to talk about anything.* Successful couples are able to talk about any subject without fear that their partner will take offence or cause a row. They do not have taboo areas that should never be openly discussed (sex and money are the main areas for trouble in couple relationships). This is not to say that they will not disagree. In fact, they probably do disagree with each other, but this disagreement is not seen as a real difficulty. They are also willing to take account of, and value, whatever their partner is saying, even if they do not entirely agree with every word.

8 *A shared sense of humour.* The ability to laugh together is often overlooked by couples, but seeing the funny side of things can often carry you through tough times. However, successful couples are those who laugh together, but not *at* each other, and who

do not tease or make fun of each other in front of friends. The art of seeing the ridiculous in a relationship can add a sense of fun to mundane daily routine.

9 *A fulfilling intimate life.* So much is written about sex that you might imagine it is the most important thing in every couple's life. The truth is that it is *one* of the important things, but not the *most* important. I have deliberately used the word 'intimate' instead of 'sex'. Sexual intercourse is not the only expression of intimacy between a couple. Sensual and sexual caressing, mutual arousal and talking about sex are all forms of intimacy that can give almost as much pleasure as intercourse. The role of non-procreative sex is thought to boost a sense of bonding to a partner, and is a real source of pleasure for most couples. Regular intimate acts have also been shown to reduce stress and aid relaxation.

10 *A willingness to try to see things from a partner's perspective.* If you can enter into your partner's world, you will be better able to understand how they see things. This does not mean you should abandon your particular opinion, but simply that you should empathise with your partner when they need you to. This quality is also important in family life in general. If you enforce rigid rules on children, without taking account of their individuality or differing circumstances, you may end up with a family of robots rather than creative human beings! This ability to look at things from another's perspective is a crucial building block for most couples. When it is missing, partners can feel alienated and frustrated and serious problems can develop in the relationship.

WHY DOES LOW COUPLE-ESTEEM OCCUR?

Now that you know what factors commonly indicate a couple with high self-esteem, you may be asking what stops this process from happening. Why is it that some couples seem to maintain a high couple-esteem, while others struggle to continue feeling good about themselves or their relationships? Tolstoy's quote (see page 159) gives us a clue. He asserts that unhappy families are usually unique in their unhappiness. This is true to at least some extent – most couples with low self-esteem will be unhappy because they have met a set of circumstances that are particular to them. But there are some shared themes that couples with low couple-esteem experience. Read the following to see if you identify with any of the indicators listed:

A lack of communication. This is the 'biggie' in relationship terms. If you cannot talk and listen to one another then none of the other things required to maintain couple-esteem can happen. You may have started the relationship by talking openly to each other, but found that this has gradually stopped, so that you now know there are emotional 'bear traps' waiting if you try to talk to one another.

A stressful lifestyle. If you are both very busy, perhaps at work, caring for children or elderly parents, you may feel that your relationship has sunk to the bottom of the list of things you need to do. Instead of being a support and source of pleasure, it becomes a chore alongside the cleaning and shopping.

A recent traumatic event. Some couples feel that their relationship takes a back seat following a traumatic event, such as a bereavement, the sickness of a family member, a job change or a financial difficulty. Or they may find that the trauma exposes pre-existing cracks in the relationship. If the after-effects of the trauma are long lasting (and they often are) the relationship can run aground under the added pressure of coping with what has happened. For instance, Charles and Sophie felt their relationship cool down when Sophie suffered a long-term illness. Sophie felt that Charles did not give the kind of support she needed, and this caused a prolonged period of arguments.

Passing through a particular 'life stage'. Life stages can come in all shapes and sizes, and affect couples differently. The most common involve growing older and other people in the family. For example, any of the following can be classed as a 'life stage': having a first child, celebrating a fortieth birthday, the death of a parent, seeing the last child leave home, passing through the menopause, and having a child start school. For example, if you are a parent who has stayed at home with small children, you may feel that your personal role has changed when they start school. This can have a knock-on effect on your relationship with your partner as you come to terms with the change you are facing.

A change in shared values. If you encounter a difference in values as your relationship progresses, you may develop a feeling that you have little in common. Your couple-esteem will slump because you are likely to find it hard to talk to one another, or feel misunderstood. This is how

Francesca and Derek felt when they disagreed about how to spend £8,000 they won on the lottery. Derek wanted to take the family on the holiday of a lifetime, while Francesca thought they should invest the cash. Neither could understand the other's attitude and instead of enjoying their good fortune they both felt thoroughly miserable. A special event (such as winning the lottery, or even a family wedding) can bring to the surface shifts in attitude in a way that might never be uncovered in other, more everyday, situations.

Personal disappointments or problems. Some couple-esteem difficulties are brought about by problems encountered by one partner. For example, a new manager at Jane's office criticised her much more often than her previous manager, with whom Jane had got on well. Jane felt she could not address the difficulty at work, but took her resentment and sadness home with her. Her partner Craig could not understand why Jane was so snappy and unlike herself. He blamed himself, and they began a period of poor communication which lasted several months until Jane told Craig of all her pent-up unhappiness at work.

IMPROVING COUPLE-ESTEEM

If you have recognised yourself in the list above, there are some steps you can take straight away to give your relationship an instant couple-esteem boost. First and most important is to begin to improve your communication skills. Here are some 'dos' and 'don'ts' for making immediate changes.

Step One

- Do put time aside to talk to one another. Turn off the TV and make sure you are reasonably relaxed and unlikely to be interrupted.
- Do tackle one subject at a time. Dragging in every issue you want to discuss is unhelpful. It is tempting to do this because you may have bottled up your thoughts for some time. Pace yourself and you will find the conversation easier to manage.
- Don't wander about the room. Try to maintain eye contact while sitting somewhere comfortable.
- Don't jump to assumptions about what your partner is saying. Give them plenty of time to finish what they are saying and then answer in a calm way.
- Do look for win/win situations, rather than trying to browbeat your partner into seeing things your way. Discuss what action should follow from your conversations, rather than spending time talking but not making a practical change.
- Do limit your talking time – half an hour is about right if you have not spent much time discussing personal issues for a while. Build up to about an hour. Otherwise you may touch on a maze of issues that only confuse you both.

Step Two

Find more time to relax and let go of the stress of everyday life. You can spend a lot of money on stress cures or try the following simple tension-releasing techniques: try going for walks together or playing simple games at the local park – kicking a ball around, playing Frisbee or tennis can all help to release muscle tension. It does not matter if you are hopeless at games. In fact, if you laugh together at your ineptitude, this will also make you feel better! Avoid competition at all costs. The object of this kind of playing around is not to see who is better at catching the ball, but to enjoy a bit of rough and tumble. Toddlers are rarely stressed in the way that adults are, so take a leaf out of their book and just mess around for the sake of it rather than to achieve some sporting triumph!

Once you have built some physical activity into your life, try de-stressing your lifestyle. Make sure you are not overworking, do not bring work home if you can avoid it and do not let work time leak into your domestic space. This is particularly difficult if you work from home, but keeping documents in a separate room or filing cabinet rather than in family living space can make all the difference. Use your answering machine to 'buy' you personal time, and avoid checking your e-mails every five minutes! It could also pay to look at your daily routines. Do you spend every day muddling through somehow rather than feeling in control of your life? If you find you argue over who will take the kids to school or who should cook the dinner, you need to do some sorting out in order to make things easier. The idea of a rota probably sounds boring and counter to what you hope a close relationship should be – a situation where both of you know by Extra Sensory Perception what the other needs. You will not be surprised to learn that this kind of relationship does not exist in real life! If you want a real sense of couple-esteem, you need to deal with the mundane facts of life in order to make time to have fun together. Establishing a routine and talking about how to create positive time together is a small price to pay.

Step Three

If you have identified problems following a traumatic event or life stage change, the most important thing to do is to acknowledge what has happened to you. Many couples experience a dive in couple-esteem because they brush difficulties under the carpet and try to go on as if nothing has happened. This tactic usually causes a great deal of trouble because suppressing emotion about something usually means it will bubble up somewhere else. Months later you may still be arguing about a seemingly unrelated event or hardly talking at all for fear that all the buried feelings will tumble out. Use the guidelines above to help you to talk about a particular event or issue.

For example, Veronica decided to talk to her husband David about his near brush with death after a serious traffic accident. David had narrowly escaped being killed in a motorway pile-up. After some time in hospital, and a fairly quick physical recovery, David returned home and was granted extended leave from work in order to convalesce. However, Veronica thought he seemed preoccupied and hard to communicate with. The first few times she tried, David pushed her away, telling her he was all right and did not need to talk. But Veronica persisted, and eventually David explained he was feeling very guilty because he had lived while others had died in the crash. They spent the next few weeks talking, on and off, about his feelings, and their relationship improved greatly. (On page 171 you will see how one partner's low self-esteem can lead to low couple-esteem.)

Step Four

Low couple-esteem can stem from taking each other for granted. You may decide that your partner's attitudes and beliefs have not changed, and perhaps continue just jogging along through everyday family life. It can then come as a shock to discover that your partner actually holds very different views from those that you thought they held. Often the exposure of this change of attitude is accompanied by recriminations as both partners try to adjust to the fact that the person they thought they knew has disappeared. Some couples tell Relate counsellors that they feel as if 'the rug has been pulled out from under us'. It is not unusual for a particular event to bring to the surface significant changes in attitude that had been previously hidden. Naz and Anna felt this way when Naz returned home from work one Friday evening to tell Anna that he had given his notice in. Anna was shocked. They had two teenage children and needed Naz's regular work as a mechanic to keep the family going. Naz told Anna that he had increasingly come to feel that his job was boring and that he felt frustrated. They went on to have a huge argument, chiefly because Naz did not seem to be able to say what he wanted to do instead of being a mechanic. Over the next few weeks, Anna became desperately worried about their financial situation. She had a part-time job as a care assistant at a residential home, but this did not bring in enough money to support them. Naz had managed to tell Anna that he wanted to retrain as a computer operator, but this would take time and money they did not have. Anna had not realised that Naz had changed his attitude to the work he had done since leaving school, and Naz had assumed that Anna would understand his reasoning. Both were pulled up short by Naz's decision.

The chief difficulty in this kind of situation is that the partner who suddenly announces a change has not shared their thought process with their partner. When the partner hears about the change of opinion (or action, as in Naz and Anna's case) they have to work very hard, first of all to change their ideas about their partner, and then to adjust to the new person in order to relate to them successfully. This process takes time and effort. If you find yourself in this kind of situation the most important thing to do is to give yourself time to think about the likely impact on your relationship or family. If you know you have changed in some way, talk to your partner as you pass through the process of change. If you can do this you will avoid some of the shock process that can follow if you tell your partner when they have little idea of what you have been thinking or planning. Once you have allowed yourself a time 'buffer zone', discuss practicalities. It may be a very small change that you wish to make – perhaps becoming a vegetarian after being a meat eater – or a larger change, such as going for promotion at work. Whatever it is, sharing your intentions with your partner will allow them to adjust and also help you to achieve your goals. Anna and Naz might have decided that Naz should carry on working as a mechanic while taking evening classes in computing, for instance. Attacking a change in small, achievable steps is far preferable to taking a giant leap into the dark, dragging an unwilling partner over the edge with you.

THE LINK BETWEEN LOW SELF-ESTEEM AND LOW COUPLE-ESTEEM

If you feel unhappy about yourself, this can, over time, lead to low couple-esteem. How you view yourself can have a dramatic effect on a couple relationship. This section will explain why this happens, and what you can do about it.

How your low self-esteem affects your partner

If you are suffering from low self-esteem you will find that this has a powerful effect on your partner. This might seem an obvious thing to say – of course, if you are feeling miserable or unhappy about some aspect of your life, your emotions will touch your partner. He or she may feel they should offer you help, or take some action to alter what is making you feel unhappy. These are all common responses to a partner's low self-esteem. But there are deeper effects. Here is how individual low self-esteem can flow through a relationship, causing low couple-esteem:

1 You feel low about yourself. This may be connected to outside circumstances – perhaps you have lost your job or feel worried about how your teenage son will support himself now he has left school, for example.

Or your loss of self-esteem could be personal –
perhaps you have gained or lost a lot of weight, feel
depressed for no apparent reason or reached the same
age that your mother was when she died. (All of these
can contribute to low self-esteem because they cause
you to question your own effectiveness, self-image and
ability to cope with life.)

2 Your partner tries to help you to feel more positive.
Perhaps they try to 'jolly you along' by telling you
that what you feel low about is not important. Or they
try to change whatever is causing your unhappiness.
For instance, they may try to persuade your son to
find a job quickly or tell you to join a slimming club.
These approaches tend not to work. Sometimes, this
'let me fix it for you' approach can actually make
things worse.

3 Your partner observes that their efforts have made
little difference. They begin to wonder if the problem
is actually their fault. Once this thought has occurred,
people tend to respond in two different ways. They
either take the blame to heart, and begin to feel low
themselves, or push the responsibility completely
towards you, with the result that you are likely to feel
worse.

4 This sense of blame, and lack of resolution, makes
both of you feel bad. If your partner blames themselves, they may seek increasingly futile ways to
make you (and themselves) feel better. This kind of
behaviour can take the form of actions designed to
resolve the situation. For instance, Vicky had a rift
with her mother which made her feel very depressed.
When her partner, Oliver, realised what had caused

Vicky's loss of esteem, he went to Vicky's mother and demanded that she make things up with Vicky. This only served to make things worse as Vicky's mother was annoyed that Vicky had not approached her in person. Vicky also felt worse, because she did not know how to deal with the angry response that followed Oliver's intervention. In fact, Oliver took the action he did because he blamed himself for not supporting Vicky more effectively when she first ran into difficulties with her mother.

Your self-esteem can be made worse by a partner who feels they do have some responsibility for your unhappiness, but cannot accept this on an emotional level. They then seek to put as much of the blame back in your court. For example, Peter noticed that Ruth was often tired and unhappy about her job at a local firm of solicitors. She frequently spent the evenings crying or sleeping. Peter felt guilty about this. He had pushed Ruth towards taking the job in the first place because it represented a better salary, although the hours were longer than Ruth had previously worked. Peter responded by telling Ruth she was 'disorganised' and it was this that spoilt her working day. Ruth privately felt she *was* disorganised, and saw Peter's comments as confirmation that she was useless at her job. Peter also felt angry towards Ruth for not coping, and she felt resentful towards Peter that he was unable to support her. Ruth not only ended up blaming herself, but also felt irritated with Peter for not helping her to decide what to do.

5 The relationship begins to feel less secure. The person with low esteem feels caught, either blaming

themselves for their feelings, or feeling blamed by their partner for their difficulties. Both partners may find themselves wondering if they can repair the damage. In some situations, the person with low self-esteem blames their partner for all their problems, and this can lead to rows and disagreements. An emotional 'pass the parcel' can begin, so that each partner either takes the blame or blames the other. With all these strong emotions running around, it is no wonder that the relationship soon begins to feel shaky. Low couple-esteem then ensues and a vicious circle begins, as the couple begin to wonder if the relationship can survive, which only adds to personal feelings of failure and sadness.

This paints a rather gloomy picture of the long-term effects of low self-esteem, but it does not have to be this way. Here are some simple steps to prevent low self-esteem leading to low couple-esteem.

- Avoid acting on your partner's behalf or telling them that they have brought all their problems on them-selves. Even if there are obvious difficulties that they need to resolve or take responsibility for, standing back and acting as a 'sounding board' is better than trying to sort out a partner's self-esteem for them. Ultimately, they will need to find the right way for-ward for themselves, preferably with your affectionate support.

- Try to help your partner to look for any possible trig-gers for the lowering of their self-esteem. If you can find any, talk about what this means to them. Be patient and attentive and they will find the words they need. Once you get talking, think about how you could change things. Avoid looking for false solutions. Just play with ideas and allow new ways of looking at old problems to emerge. This may take some time, but there is no instant remedy to help someone to feel good about themselves.

- Watch out for your reaction. Note if you feel everything must be your fault, or if your partner in some way deserves all the miserable feelings they are experiencing. This may be a form of defence to prevent you feeling an emotional response to your partner's low esteem.

- Look for things to do that help you to feel close to each other as a couple. Make a list of all the things you enjoy – antique hunting, going to the cinema, having a quiet night in, walking by the sea or in the park – and arrange to do at least one of these once a week. This is really important, as these special events can help the relationship to maintain its couple-esteem even if one partner has low self-esteem.

- If your partner feels really low, they may, in an emotional sense, lash out at you. (Chapter 9 contains a section on aggression in relationships, and its roots in low self-esteem.) They may blame you for everything that has gone wrong, or simply be snappy and uncommunicative. In this situation, try hard to support your partner. Reflect what they are actually saying or doing. Try 'I can see you are angry/upset/miserable about. . .' or, 'You seem very unhappy/irritable/unsettled'. Reflecting back what you observe can help because it gives a clear picture to your partner of what they are giving out. Doing this can also help you to understand that the emotions belong to your partner and are not necessarily yours. Invest some time in thinking what *you* really feel as this will enable you to remain objective, but not disconnected, from your partner.

- Keep reminding each other of what brought you together, how special you are for each another and what hopes you have for the future. This can be really important if you are having a tough time. Recalling good times, and trying to recreate these in the present, can make a positive difference. Revisit old haunts or find new places you would like to visit, watch films you both enjoy, listen to favourite music – do anything that boosts your mutual bond.

IN CONCLUSION

This chapter has allowed you to assess your relationship and try different approaches to improving couple-esteem. It has also demonstrated how low personal self-esteem leads to low couple-esteem, and how this can be rectified so that the relationship can survive a slump in the self-esteem of one partner.

Chapter 8

SEXUAL RELATIONSHIPS AND COUPLE-ESTEEM

It is possible to have sex without a relationship, and a relationship without sex, but for most people the ideal is to have a relationship that contains intimacy and sex in an appropriate balance for the individuals concerned. It is perhaps surprising that as a society that promotes sex in advertising, on TV and films, in newspapers and magazines, on the internet, and even to sell cars, we still find it hard to have fulfilling sexual relationships. Every magazine is full of letters from people who feel their sex life is not as they would want it to be, or contain articles on how to improve sex.

Why is sex so important in couple relationships? And how can it lower or lift couple-esteem? After all, many single people exist happily in a celibate state. Here are some reasons why sex is thought to be important in couple relationships (other than for procreation!).

- *Sex is fun.* If most of your life is taken up with activities designed to pay the bills, or caring for a growing family, sex can be an excellent stress reliever, giving couples a little oasis in which to relax and to escape the strains of everyday life. An overlooked attribute of satisfying sex is that it is possible to lose yourself in it, in the same way that you can lose yourself in a good book, an exciting piece of music or an 'edge-of-your-seat' film.

- *Sex is bonding*. It has been a puzzle for some time as to why human beings continue to have sexual relationships even when they do not wish to procreate. Putting aside the pure physical pleasure of sex, it is thought that regular sex has a bonding element to it. The shared touching and caressing and sexual satisfaction help the couple to feel 'as one', and this can be a circular process – the more regular, good-quality sex you have, the closer you feel to one another and the more you desire sexual contact.

- *Sex is comforting*. It may be a surprising thought, but sexual contact after a traumatic event can help both partners to feel cared for and loved. This may mimic the intimacy babies feel when being breast-fed or being held by a parent. Most people crave the affection of another after a devastating experience, and sex between two people who are suffering can say 'I love and care for you' in a special way. This kind of sex is not usually madly passionate, but gentle and comforting.

- *Sex is a conversation*. Sometimes a couple can use their sexual relationship to express affection. Intimate touching, the feel of warm skin and passionate kisses can all tell your partner how much you love them in a uniquely personal way. As in all conversations, some exchanges will be deep and full of meaning, while others will be short and jokey. This kind of communication is like an extended conversation that can last for years, and brings with it a profound depth to a relationship.

- *Sex is forgiveness.* This aspect of sexual relationships is not widely acknowledged, but sexual contact can help to heal pain in a loving relationship. Many couples report that after a flaming row they end up in bed. Perhaps this is linked to the emotional intensity that arguing brings to the fore, or because the couple need to reinvigorate their 'bonding' (see opposite), but it is a well known phenomenon. Allowing another to touch the most intimate places of your body requires openness. If this happens after a disagreement, it can demonstrate your willingness to open up to your partner, and to reflect on what has happened, rather than closing off your heart and mind. Sometimes this kind of sex is accompanied by tears, or a kind of roughness that can feel exciting, but also a bit frightening. This is natural, but you probably would not want this kind of sex all the time.

COMMON SEXUAL PROBLEMS

Given that sex can incorporate all the important facets listed above, how is it that couples can run into sexual problems that lower their couple-esteem? Here are some common sexual difficulties that can lead to low couple-esteem:

- *You develop sexual 'crossed wires'.* If one partner is looking for sex that is simply fun and not too emotionally demanding, while the other is looking for sex that is all-consuming, the couple may feel out of step. For example, Yola and her husband Sergei had been married for 18 months when their sex life began to falter. Yola felt that Sergei treated their love life in a way that did not reflect their commitment to one another. He often pushed for sex, and sometimes took little notice of her need to be aroused or to reach a climax. In one angry exchange she told Sergei he behaved as if she was 'a one-night stand'. Sergei found it hard to understand what Yola was saying – the sex was satisfying to him, and it did not cross his mind to consider that Yola might want more from him.

- *You have differing sexual appetites.* This can be an immediately obvious problem once you begin your sexual relationship, or develop over the months and years that you are together. It can also follow a particular life stage – after childbirth, for instance. Characteristically, one partner becomes the pursuer, constantly asking for, or trying to initiate, sex, while the other partner becomes the hunted, often backing off from love making, or simply avoiding the subject. A common scenario is where one partner goes to bed, hoping the other will soon arrive so they can make love, while the other, recognising this, stays downstairs watching TV until the small hours of the morning. The more pressure the pursuer puts on the pursued, the less the hunted wants sex. In fact, the gap in appetite will grow the more pressure is applied until a there is a kind of hatred of any mention of sex. At this point the couple are likely to feel very low in couple-esteem, perhaps seeing themselves as failures in a society where everyone is supposed to 'be at it'.

- *You find sex boring.* Many couples report that sex *can* be boring. This often happens after the initial intense phase of passion that couples encounter at the start of a relationship. As things settle down, and they have to take on the less starry-eyed aspects of being together – like cleaning a shared house or arguing over who should cook the evening meal – sex also begins to seem rather flat. This is because the sexual act becomes distanced from the two people actually doing it, and becomes more like a routine where the partners feel anonymous. The way to counter this difficulty is to view sex as a creative act (not just for creating babies).

- *Sex becomes a power game.* Many couples with low esteem tell Relate counsellors that, for them, sex has become a power game – that is, they used sex to try to manipulate a partner or a situation. For example, Kelly knew that withdrawing sex from her boyfriend, Keith, could make him do what she wanted. He would find himself feeling guilty that he had not been more understanding and would try to win her round. In these circumstances, some people become angry or withdraw, but many couples feel that using sex in this way can achieve an emotional goal that cannot be scored in any other way. Some partners ridicule each other sexually or give sex as an emotional 'reward' for 'good behaviour' by their partner. In some bizarre situations, couples will give sex for tasks undertaken, such as tiling the bathroom, or a favour granted, such as allowing a partner to have a night out with their mates. In this situation, all real feeling is drained from love-making. It becomes a charade which can, in turn, lead to serious sexual problems, or sexual dysfunctions, as they are sometimes called (see page 182).

Other sexual problems can result from these situations and in overcoming them Relate Psychosexual Therapy can be extremely helpful. You can make an appointment to see a Psychosexual Therapist at your local Relate centre. Look in your local *Yellow Pages* or check out the Relate website www.relate.org.uk . If you recognise any of the problems below, consider seeking the help of Relate:

Male sexual difficulties	Female sexual difficulties
General loss of/lack of interest in sex – a feeling that there is little sex drive, accompanied by feelings of apathy about initiating sex.	General loss of/lack of interest in sex – see male loss of interest.
Erectile problems – any problem relating to achieving and keeping an erection. Can occur at any time in a relationship.	Orgasm problems – may never have (or have had) an orgasm, or reaches orgasm during masturbation but not with a partner, or can achieve orgasm during love play with a partner but not during intercourse.
Premature ejaculation – ejaculating during foreplay or just on entry to the vagina or after a brief time inside the vagina.	Vaginismus – unable to accept a penis into the vagina. Caused by an involuntary clenching of the muscles at the entrance to the vagina. The woman may also feel unable to use tampons or to put a finger inside the vagina.
Delayed ejaculation – an erection is kept but after prolonged stimulation (inter vaginally or by hand) the man does not ejaculate or does so only after an extremely long time.	Dyspareunia – sexual intercourse is painful, often as the penis enters the vagina. Pain may also occur deeper inside the vagina or at the cervix.

All of these things can cause, or be the result of, low couple-esteem. If you think you have experienced these it is important to see your GP in the first instance to rule out any obvious physical causes. For example, some medications or diseases can cause loss of erection. Dyspareunia can be caused by physical difficulties, such as poorly healed stitches after childbirth, that should be sorted out before attempting therapy. All Relate therapists are trained to look for the symptoms of physical problems and will help with GP referral if you would like this.

IMPROVING COUPLE SEXUAL ESTEEM

If you have met any of the difficulties outlined above you will know how quickly they can lower your couple and self-esteem. Even if sex is not particularly important to you, difficulties with the sex life you have chosen can quickly become a sparking point for arguments and recriminations. There are some simple steps you can take to improve things quickly. If you follow these, you can move on to try some of the longer term recovery steps listed later in the chapter.

Instant sexual healing

- Stop trying to make love at the end of a long tiring day. Nothing is more likely to lead to sexual strife. Shift love-making to early evening, early morning or any other time when you can be alone and relaxed.
- If you feel sex has become a pressure, try agreeing to

stop attempting intercourse for a short while – say a week or two (but stick to this agreed time span – no shorter or longer). In the intervening time, give each other massages, take showers together, cuddle and kiss and experiment with new kinds of love play.

- Women often suffer from lack of interest in sex. New research suggests that most women, of all ages, are on a 10-day cycle of sexual interest. Ask your partner to stop asking or otherwise pressurising you for sex and wait to see if your sexual feelings return. You may need to wait at least a week without sexual contact, but many women report that their natural desire begins to surface after about seven days. In fact, the reason you may not want to make love could be because there has not been enough emotional space for you to connect with your natural cycle of sexual desire. Given this space, your desire may well reappear.

- Agree a 'love pact' with your partner. Decide that you will have *at least* half an hour of caressing and intimate touching before you begin to think about intercourse. Fast sex is often unfulfilling sex. Slowing things down can be very helpful.

- Make a list of all the things you want from sex. Include all the emotional things as well as the physical. Ask your partner if they share your desires. For example, Richard wrote the following on his list:
  - ✓ Feeling of closeness to Louise (his partner)
  - ✓ More touching on parts of my body aside from my genitals
  - ✓ To have the light on more often during sex
  - ✓ For Louise to tell me what she likes about my body

✓ To hear Louise say 'I love you' and to say it back to her

✓ To make love in the lounge

✓ For Louise to initiate sex sometimes

✓ To give Louise an orgasm when we have sex

✓ To cuddle and talk after sex rather than just going straight to sleep

✓ For Louise to tell me more about what she enjoys when we make love

This kind of list can be really helpful because it allows you both to reflect on what is good about your shared sex and what could be improved.

- Take a break away. This may sound like a cliché, but taking time to be alone as just a couple (rather than 'mum and dad' or 'Mr and Ms career couple') can be just what you need to rejuvenate your sexual relationship. If you can afford it, a week in a favourite holiday resort is ideal, but a weekend can be just as good. If you cannot take this kind of break, perhaps for financial reasons or parenting concerns, try to ensure that you have one weekend every three months that is full of things that you both really enjoy – including love-making. Stay in bed for sensual lie-ins and have early nights. If someone you trust will look after the children, you can still have a sexy weekend in your own home!

- Revisit sexy things you enjoyed when you began your sexual relationship. If you enjoyed dressing up for sex, do it again! It is easy to forget things that aroused you in the early days and settle into routine sex that is over in less than 15 minutes. Use your erotic memories to inspire your imagination.

LONGER-TERM SEXUAL RECOVERY

You may find that you have deeper sexual problems that require other solutions. This section deals with some of the longer term issues that can lead to low couple esteem.

Common problems that can lead to long-term sexual problems

Unresolved anger

Many couples find that their sex life is damaged by anger that simmers under the surface of their partnership. This kind of anger is often not characterised by rows or angry explosions, but becomes a chronic irritation. If you feel this way, it can eventually degrade every part of your relationship, including sex. For example, Lewis and Sonia found that their sexual relationship diminished over a period of months after Sonia lost her job. Lewis blamed Sonia for losing her job as a machinist because of her poor time keeping. He knew that the firm had warned her she ran the risk of losing her job if she did not arrive on time, but she still often slept in, missing her bus in the morning. Lewis was extremely worried about their financial situation, while Sonia felt another job would eventually come along. During this period, Lewis felt distant from, and cold towards, Sonia, and their sex life suffered as a consequence. Angry feelings can be triggered in this way by a specific event, or seem to permeate the relationship because of a multitude of dissatisfactions.

Managing anger

Dealing with long-term feelings of anger can free up your sexual relationship. Here is how to stop anger interfering with your intimate relationship:

- Look for the trigger to your anger. Do you know how it started? Is it just one event or several?
- If it helps, write down your ideas and feelings about why you (and your partner) feel angry with one another.
- Find time to talk to each other about what has happened. It is possible that you will have an argument, but this may be a catalyst to stopping the anger bubbling under the surface. If you do argue, do not walk out. Try to look for solutions afterwards, and be honest about what you expect from each other. Lewis, for example, could ask Sonia to look for a job more enthusiastically.
- Discuss solutions to issues that may have been around for a long time. Once you have found ways of sorting out these irritations, keep a list somewhere that you compiled jointly. For instance, if you both agree to keep the kitchen tidier or to take turns to pick the children up from school, stick to your agreement.
- Invest time in rebuilding your sexual relationship. Do not wait for your partner to suggest making love – take the initiative yourself and make a special date and time when you will make love.

Lack of trust

If your relationship is fairly new, problems with sex and trust can simply take time to sort out as you grow to know more about your partner. It is usually better to take a new sexual relationship slowly, rather than jumping into bed within a few days or weeks of meeting a new partner. Lack of trust can also follow after a specific event, such as an affair. Trust, once broken, can take a long time to repair. If you find it hard to trust a partner, it is almost certain that your sex life will suffer. This is because allowing a partner to see and touch you at your most vulnerable requires a great deal of trust, an absence of which will probably cause you to feel extremely uncomfortable. In this situation, most people want to curl up like a hedgehog and defend themselves from further perceived emotional attack. (However, occasionally the converse can be true. A partner who feels in danger of losing their lover may try to become extremely seductive in a bid to hang onto him or her.)

Managing lack of, and rebuilding, trust

- It is crucial to discuss what led to the lack of trust. Gloria and Brian found that they avoided sex after Gloria discovered that Brian had had a drunken snog with a work colleague at a Christmas party. Although nothing like a full-blown affair, Gloria still felt let down by Brian's behaviour. Every time she tried to have sex, she thought of Brian kissing the woman in the office. Gloria and Brian avoided talking about what had happened, but this response is a mistake. Talking about the event and trying to make sense of its significance is extremely important because it can help you both to understand why it has affected you in the way it has.

- Tell each other what you want to happen now. Trust is in the proof, not the promise. If you can actually decide to carry out practical changes, it can help the slow rebuilding of trust. For example, Gloria asked Brian always to come back from the office on time. Brian asked Gloria not to drag up the incident in every disagreement.

- Always apologise for any behaviour that has harmed your relationship. This is not only applicable to your partner but also applies to you. This will involve getting to grips with anything that you think has contributed to the problem in the first place. Honestly facing up to personal responsibilities can help you both to banish the trigger that caused the breakdown of trust, instead of just patching up a difficult situation.

Anxiety

Anxiety can take many forms. For some people it feels omnipresent, as if they can never escape the overwhelming worries of their everyday life. For others, anxiety is short-lived, and often related to something special – such as waiting for an exam result. Anxiety – often linked to stress and tiredness – has the potential to damage sexual relationships dramatically. It can have a physiological effect – such as loss of erection or lack of lubrication – or a psychological effect – leading to irritability and lack of concentration. Chronic anxiety may indicate that you have a real problem in trusting your partner and need to seek Relate counselling.

Managing anxiety

- The physical effects of anxiety can make any situation seem much worse. Tension headaches, stomach aches and stiff muscles will all contribute to a feeling that everything is on top of you. You can counteract this by taking some regular physical exercise – a daily walk is a good start, or even using an exercise video on a regular basis. Swimming is also helpful as it encourages you to breathe in a deeper, more relaxed way. Anxiety often causes shallow breathing that can lead to stressful hyperventilation. (See Chapters 3 and 5 for more information about exercise and anxiety.)

- As with lack of trust (see page 187) look for the trigger to your anxiety problems. If you can solve your concern at root, your anxiety will fade away.

- Try to change what you can and stop worrying about what is unchangeable. Take action on those things that can be tackled, and shelve anything that is beyond your control. For example, Evelyn worried about her husband's heart condition and found love making very difficult to enjoy because she feared her husband would have a heart attack. When he discovered her worry, he made them both an appointment with their GP who explained the unlikelihood of this happening.

- If your anxiety is linked to something you know is inevitable, ask your partner for plenty of affectionate reassurance. For example, Tracy was mentally and physically worn out with caring for her dying father and felt that sex was the last thing on her mind. She explained this to her partner, Rob, and asked him to just hold her as she went to sleep. Rob understood that Tracy's anxiety would eventually diminish, and was able to respond to her need for warmth and emotional support at the level she requested.

Sex may not be the central plank of your relationship, but many couples know the negative effect that lack of intimacy can cause. Maintaining an affectionate life together and enjoying sensuous love making can help you both to feel that the relationship is worth investing in, as well as improving your personal self-esteem.

IN CONCLUSION

This chapter has looked at why sexual relationships have an important effect on couple-esteem. Some quick solutions to sexual problems have been suggested, as well as longer-term ones. All sexual relationships can be affected by outside circumstances, such as tiredness and anxiety, but maintaining a fulfilling sexual relationship can make a positive contribution to couple-esteem.

Chapter 9

WHEN LOVING ANOTHER HURTS

The common image of romantic love is of both partners instinctively understanding and fulfilling each other's needs and desires. Eventually, so the dream tells us, the couple will live a life of mutual understanding. But for many people this is just a fantasy. Real couple relationships are made up of times when both partners feel in tune, and other times when they feel completely alienated. Feeling close and in tune can last for months, a day or an hour, as can feeling alienated. All relationships are affected by life stages – choosing to have (or not have) children, caring for parents or other elderly relatives, career ups and downs, maturing. All of this is to be expected in a loving relationship for no more complex reason than that we are all human – prey to faults and failings as well as moments of great generosity.

Some couples encounter further difficulties that put their relationship under great strain. Far from the partnership meeting their expectations at least some of the time, most of the time is spent trying to rescue the relationship from certain breakdown, or trying to understand why a partner has behaved in a hurtful manner. In other words, trying to make sense of why loving another hurts so much. There are lots of reasons why loving can hurt. Many of them are unique to each couple and are brought about by particular events in their lives. Others are well known to Relate counsellors, and often crop up in relationships where pain and sadness are common denominators.

Common situations that cause hurt in relationships

Lack of respect

If your partner does not respect you, you may feel as if you are not a real person. You may find that your partner does not take your feelings into account, or behaves towards you in a thoughtless and irresponsible manner.

Case Study

Loreena and Dexter had lived together for five years when Loreena found herself wondering if they could go on together. Dexter often spent whole nights out with his friends, not returning until the following day. On one memorable occasion, he disappeared for three days without contacting her. Loreena also felt that she did far more than her fair share of looking after the flat they shared. She frequently tried to get Dexter to think about her, and had left him at least four times, only to return when he came looking for her, promising to change his ways. Loreena cared for Dexter – when he was not behaving in a careless way she liked his sense of humour and shared his musical tastes. But she was extremely hurt by his attitude towards

*her, feeling more like an object he picked up and put down
when it suited him, rather than a partner who should be
accorded respect. After a huge showdown, during which
Dexter told her he did not care if she stayed or went,
Loreena packed her bags and left. This time she felt determined to end the relationship straight away.*

Feeling that a partner fundamentally lacks respect for
you can wear down a relationship until there is almost
nothing left. If you find you keep going back to such a
relationship, you will eventually have to answer a crucial
question – why? People do face this question regularly.
Something seems to hold them, even when friends and
relatives tell them that the relationship is emotionally
(and sometimes physically) damaging. The most common answer to this difficult question is that they have
such a low opinion of themselves that they feel they
almost deserve the treatment they are receiving. This is a
bitter pill to swallow. It is hard to admit, even to yourself, that you do not feel confident of finding a partner
who will really value you. You may also enjoy the 'roller-
coaster' effect of relationships that are characterised by
storms. But although this style may seem attractive,
suggesting that you are a passionate couple who are not
ready for the easy life yet, after some years of extreme
highs and lows, you can find yourself emotionally
exhausted, longing for some security and commitment. If
this scenario sounds familiar, there are some important
questions you should ask yourself. Try writing the
following questions down, and then answering the
questions on the same page. Be honest, and try to face
the truth about how you feel.

1   Why do I stay in this relationship?
2   What I am afraid of if I leave?
3   What kind of relationship would I really like? Can I achieve this in my present relationship? How?
4   What would I need to do to have a relationship that is more respectful?
5   What would my partner need to do to demonstrate respect towards me?
6   Are there any hidden psychological 'benefits' that I gain from staying in my present relationship? (For example, 'If I stay, although I am unhappy, I might be protected from facing my fear that no one else would find me loveable'.)
7   I would like to tell my partner. . . (write down anything important you wish you could say about your feelings when you are disrespected).
8   When this relationship began I wanted. . . (write down any hopes or expectations you had that have not been met).
9   I think my partner wanted. . . (try to guess what your partner wanted at the start of the relationship).
10 How will I feel if my relationship goes on in the same way for years?

Now that you have read and answered the questions and statements above, look at any surprises you have discovered. For example, Loreena might have found that she entered the partnership with Dexter with high hopes of making a success of it, but had not noticed that this expectation had been gradually worn down as things deteriorated until she had no expectations at all. Alternatively, you might identify actions you could take to improve your partnership quickly. Using questions in this way can help you to reflect on why there is a lack of respect in your partnership, and what you would like to do about the problem.

Jealousy

Some jealousy in a relationship is to be expected. In fact, occasional, mild shows of jealousy can be a sweet reminder that your partner wants and cares for you. But jealousy that eats away at you, that stops you living a normal life because you find it hard to trust your partner, or jealousy that makes you feel violent or aggressive is not at all the same. This kind of jealousy is destructive and damaging. No relationship can survive one, or both, partners behaving in an extremely jealous way. Far from enabling both partners to feel secure and safe, it usually indicates a serious lack of security that could boil over into a very dangerous situation.

Case Study

Anu and Winston had a close relationship that seemed very happy until Anu had their first child, a little boy. Winston changed jobs at around the same time as the birth, and began travelling much further to the office where he was a sales manager. Anu found being a mother much harder than she imagined. She missed Winston, who was not able to spend as much time with her in the evenings because of the extra commuting, and often felt lonely. When Winston began to talk about his colleagues, Anu became fixed on the notion that Winston preferred his secretary, Moira, to her. She began to question Winston every day about Moira. What did they talk about? What did Moira wear? Was Moira flirting with Winston? From asking this kind of question, Anu progressed to accusing Winston of having an affair or secretly seeing Moira when he went out. Winston could not convince Anu that he was simply working. He felt distressed that Anu was behaving so strangely, and upset that she did not appear to trust him. They began to argue, often ending in Anu making worse accusations. One morning when Winston was about to leave, he discovered that the doors had all been locked and he could not get out. Anu admitted locking him in and refused to let him go because she was convinced he was seeing Moira. Winston broke down in tears, and Anu realised with a jolt that she had gone beyond what was considered normal behaviour. As they slowly tried to recover, and sought the help of their GP, their relationship needed a great deal of work to be restored to anything like how it had been before Anu had their son. The GP diagnosed post-natal depression and suggested that Anu have a mild anti-depressant, while they both booked time with a surgery-based counsellor to work on their marriage.

Jealousy can eat away at a relationship, sometimes imperceptibly, until a corner is turned that allows both partners see that what has been happening is destructive. Jealousy also begets jealousy. A little jealousy can feed ideas about a partner's infidelity so that even if the jealous partner starts by having just a few concerns, they can spiral out of control as each doubt leads to further doubts. Coping with jealousy takes time – it is not easy to work on because in order to feel jealous the individual has to weave a complicated alternative reality around themselves, and then allow themselves to believe the fantasy they have created. Here are some simple pointers to help you to cope with jealousy, and Relate counselling can often help to uncover the true reasons for jealous behaviour.

- Develop a strong sense of self-esteem (see the first section of this book). If you feel good about yourself you are much less likely to feel jealous. Jealousy is a complicated emotion because jealous people almost want to feed off others who appear successful or happy, but also resent their ability to do well in life (hence situations like Anu and Winston). If you feel that your life is worth living and have goals you would like to achieve, jealousy has no room to flourish.

- If you have to deal with a partner's jealousy, recognise that you cannot humour them by meeting all their demands. The more you obey their demands, the more demands they will make. Instead, be honest about what you are doing, keep any promises you make, but explain that life is not always predictable. For example, if you find yourself stuck in a traffic jam and unable to return home at an allotted time, your partner needs to understand this. If the jealousy becomes invasive of your normal life, consider seeking extra help in order to unravel where the feelings are coming from.

- Jealousy can be an indicator of a deep insecurity in the relationship. Although one partner may show the jealousy, the insecurity can be part of a problem that is shared by both partners, but not discussed. For instance, Emma felt very disturbed by Graham's jealousy of her close friend, Mary. Graham tried to get Emma to promise that she would not see Mary, but Emma refused. As the jealousy affected more and more of their relationship, Emma and Graham realised that, in fact, the jealousy came from a feeling that they were not as emotionally close as Mary and Emma, and that this was a problem that had existed in the relationship for the two years they had been together. To some extent, try to use the jealousy as a diagnostic. Ask yourself if the jealousy is acting as a smoke screen to mask real issues that should be addressed in the partnership.

Aggression

Of all the problems that can lead to low couple-esteem, aggression is the most difficult to cope with. It has the potential to destroy a relationship very quickly. Aggression usually means intimidating looks, verbal abuse, threats, bullying and mental cruelty in the form of belittling or taunting a partner. Traditionally, this kind of behaviour is from a man towards a woman, but can also be from a woman towards a man. Some individuals endure aggression on a regular basis, often when it is linked to a partner's alcohol problem. For others it is an event that is less predictable, but nevertheless very frightening. Whenever it happens, it is the sign of a relationship in serious trouble because it indicates a serious lack of trust and empathy from the aggressor to their partner.

Case Study

Paul and Fay had been married for four months when Paul began to bully Fay. Fay was amazed by his seeming change in character. They had had a holiday romance and married quickly, feeling very infatuated with each other. At first, Paul seemed charming, but then began to insult Fay. At first he made fun of her figure, telling her she was getting fat and needed to diet. Then he demanded that she

take on most of the housework 'because this was what
women were supposed to do'. Over a period of several
months he made Fay's life a misery. He prevented her
from watching anything she chose on TV as he said she
was not allowed to choose because 'men should make all
the choices in their own homes'. He threw meals at the
kitchen wall if he did not want to eat them and insisted
she hand over her wages from her job. Fay was deeply
unhappy. She had married later in life than she had
expected, and had a dream that her marriage would be
perfect. Instead, she became desperate to hide from Paul,
and feared that one day he would physically attack her.

Coping with aggression

Most aggression comes from fear – the fear of the inst-
igator that they do not measure up or that their partner
will eventually realise that they are not 'good enough' and
leave them. It is also fed by the fear of the person on the
receiving end, as this is the 'reward' the aggressor receives
for their cruelty. If you are caught in this situation, here
are some first steps to help you to think about whether the
relationship is salvageable or if you should end it.

- Never ignore first signs of aggression. If a partner is
  rude, or begins bullying, explain firmly that you do
  not like this kind of behaviour. Do not shout or make
  demands. Just calmly state that you do not expect the
  behaviour to happen again.
- If aggression continues, say what you will do if it
  recurs. (Do not threaten your own aggression as this
  will only make things much worse.) For example, if
  you think you would go to your parents or stay with a

friend, say this. Draw a line on the behaviour. If it is repeated, carry out what you have said you will do.

- If the aggression escalates, perhaps because the tone becomes more threatening or the aggression happens more often, tell other people what is happening and make yourself safe. Unfortunately, placating your partner could act as a green light to carry on as before.
- If you want to talk to your partner, be clear about how you want the behaviour to change. For example, Fay could have told Paul she wanted him to stop being rude to her or belittling her cooking. If Paul chose not to take account of her feelings, this would give Fay a powerful message about the future of the relationship. Most people would realise that no relationship could continue with this kind of pressure.

Some aggression follows a well known pattern which makes it more difficult to counter. The common pattern looks like this:

1 Aggression takes place – verbal or emotional.
2 The person who was aggressive makes promises to never repeat the behaviour. They may give their partner gifts or try to make amends in some other way.
3 The partner believes that the act of aggression will never happen again. They begin to relax as a 'honeymoon period' begins.
4 The partner who was aggressive gradually becomes tense. Some aggressive remarks begin to creep back into their conversation.
5 The aggression is repeated.

The difficulty for the partner on the receiving end of this is that they may like the person their partner is at phase

2, but hate the partner they become at phases 1 and 5. This pattern can explain why women with aggressive male partners do not leave when most friends and relations think they should – they are simply hoping (often against all the evidence) that their partner will stay at phase 2 one day. If you have identified with this pattern, you need to consider whether you can cope with this repetition of hope, which is then destroyed, for (possibly several) years. This situation is made more complex by children and/or other dependants, but it is important to take into account the serious negative affect that witnessing aggression between parents can have on young minds.

If you regularly experience aggression it is easy to become caught in the belief that this is how your relationship has turned out, and you must tolerate it. If you find yourself thinking in this way, reflect on a relationship known to you that you admire. For instance, you may have a friend that has a warm and loving relationship, or a relative who seems to have a high self-esteem because of the loving support of their partner. Use their example to allow yourself to believe that not all relationships are characterised by threats or bullying. This can help you to shift your thinking from 'I should tolerate this behaviour' to 'I do not have to tolerate this behaviour', allowing you to realise that you too deserve a relationship that is supportive and caring rather than one that is characterised by fear or anxiety. If you take this psychological step, you will be on the way to gaining the confidence you need, and this will help you to take the appropriate action to stop the aggression you are experiencing.

Although this chapter has dealt with some of the most

difficult aspects of couple relationships, it is often possible to recover from difficult situations that cause low
couple-esteem. Talking, and then taking appropriate
action at an early stage if these kinds of difficulties
emerge, can really make a big difference. If you try to
sweep a problem under the carpet, it can eventually
become very difficult to resolve. Consider using the
advice in this chapter to stop a tough situation becoming
terrible.

IN CONCLUSION

This chapter has looked at situations that have the
potential to break a relationship. Various strategies for
dealing with especially problematic issues are given, as
well as different approaches to help you reflect on
whether the relationship should continue.

AFTERWORD

Now that you have read this book I hope you will feel that your self-esteem is not just something you are born with, but is something that you can develop and nurture so that your experiences of life can be relished rather than endured. Most people would say that their sense of self-worth ebbs and flows, according to what has happened to them or their mood. But, as I hope this book has shown you, this does not mean you have to believe old messages about not being good enough or just accept what others tell you about yourself. Through reading this book I hope you will feel able to believe in yourself, as well as understand more about what causes low or high self-esteem and act on what you have learnt.

You will also have learnt about couple-esteem. Couple-esteem can make the difference between feeling that your relationship is merely surviving and feeling that your partnership really works well.

The book encourages you to reflect on how you handle your physical, mental and emotional well being. There are no right answers – no exam to pass – that will demonstrate, once and for all, that you are a person with a positive sense of self-worth. But through answering the questions, contemplating how you presently handle difficult situations and perhaps identifying with the case studies, I hope you will discover the self- and couple-esteem that is right for you. If you find a balance that suits you and your partner, this book will have achieved what it set out to do.

I would like to offer you every good wish for the future – both for you as an individual and for your present or future relationships.

INDEX